# HE IS LORD

**Michael Cole**

**HODDER AND STOUGHTON**
LONDON SYDNEY AUCKLAND TORONTO

Unless stated otherwise, all the Bible references are taken from the New International Version of the Bible (Hodder & Stoughton 1980)

**British Library Cataloguing in Publication Data**

Cole, Michael, *1934–*
  He is Lord.—(Hodder Christian paperbacks)
  1. Christian life
  I. Title
  248'.5      BV4509.5

  ISBN 0 340 41498 7

# CONTENTS

# ACKNOWLEDGEMENTS

Many people and a number of churches have shared with me in the months during which *He is Lord* was being written. Much of the material was shared with our own church in one way or another. I am also grateful to St Saviour's, Guildford, to St Luke's, Maidstone, and to Christ Church, Ware, for opportunities to work out with them some aspects of the lordship of Jesus.

Individuals have given me incalculable help. Monica Mattock, Mark and Caroline Philps and Pamela and Stephen Evans, together with Ian Sparks, have made most valuable contributions, suggestions and – I hope – improvements to the text. Caroline Armitage, Rob Warner and David Wavre – past and present staff at Hodders – have encouraged me in many ways. Edward England and John Truscott have given me permission to quote from *Renewal* and *Administry*. Jackie and Norman Arnold – my secretary and her husband – have burnt the midnight oil in typing, retyping and producing the manuscript, and Jean Skelton has meticulously checked it. The wardens and people at All Saints' have given me time to write and have supported me in prayer. To every person I am most thankful.

It must be my wife, Stephanie, however, to whom I give my greatest acknowledgement and to whom I dedicate this book – my second – for all her love, patience and understanding as I wrote, and as together we tried to understand more of what the lordship of Jesus means.

May our combined efforts have given birth to a book worthy of the Lord himself, one which will stimulate churches and individuals in many places to honour Jesus as their Lord from now until he comes again.

December 1986                                    Michael Cole

# PREFACE

I wish I had known twenty-five years ago what I know now!

I became a committed Christian in my early teens, worked in the Civil Service after leaving school, was called to the ministry of the Church of England, and served in some exciting parishes in the North of England – in Leeds, Sheffield and Manchester. I had also spent three years working among students in universities and colleges. I knew that Jesus Christ was Lord, but I did not fully understand what this meant, or how it should work out in practice in a local church or in daily living.

Then, during a period of sabbatical leave in 1984, I was able to visit churches in the United States, Singapore, Australia and New Zealand. I was especially helped by attending a lay leadership weekend at St Paul's Church, Darien, near New York. There I heard the Rector, the Rev. Terry Fullam, spell out what it meant in practical terms for Jesus to be head of his church.

As I continued to visit, to read more widely and to reflect, I found various guidelines for the effective leadership of churches emerging. I chose to preach and teach upon these themes when I returned to the pulpit at All Saints' Church in May and June 1984.

We began to work out these truths with joy and with tears. The tears came when I tried to plan things and run them my way, resulting in tension and division rather than in unity and progress under the headship of the Lord.

There came a point in October and November 1984 where my lay leaders suggested that we needed a fresh vision from the Lord of what he wanted us to be doing. (The guidelines I had discovered helped us to understand the 'How' of church life and membership, but now he was leading us on to the 'What' of church life.) Not knowing how to receive a fresh vision and anointing from the Lord, we called the church to a time of prayer, setting aside the period of 13–19 January 1985 for just that purpose. It seemed a long way ahead, but it gave us time to prepare the congregation for it, explaining to them carefully and without hurry why we had decided to have a week of prayer, and what we would be doing during that time.

During the two main Sunday services on 13 January we focused on the week of prayer. The main central and corporate events were to be a day of prayer on the Wednesday and a half-night of prayer on the Friday. Provision was also made for one or two additional smaller meetings for prayer, and we hoped that individual members of the church would set aside time to pray and seek the Lord in the quiet of their homes during the week.

Wednesday 16 January 1985 had been set aside for group and personal prayer at home or in the church. Suggestions had been made about how best to use the time, and how to seek the Lord. There were specific issues about which we wanted to know the Lord's mind: we were concerned about the growth of our daughter church, St Andrew's; the outreach to the adults and young people in the next twelve to eighteen months; the development of the healing ministry; the need to strengthen the work of the Sunday schools among both the children and their parents; we needed to produce more home-grown leaders, and we faced the need to increase our giving.

What we thought might result from the week of prayer differed from what the Lord had in mind!

Two or three times during the previous few years God had spoken to us from Revelation 3:14–22, from the letter to the church at Laodicea. That church was saying of itself and to itself: 'I am rich; I have acquired wealth and do not need a thing.' We had unconsciously adopted a similar attitude towards ourselves, but God's view of us was very different. He had been trying to tell us that we needed to repent. We were willing to repent, but we did not know of what we had to repent, nor were we sure how to repent. The Lord showed us clearly on that Wednesday night. We needed to repent of the failure to make Jesus the Lord and head of All Saints' Church. We had to turn away from pride and self-confidence and the feeling that we were really doing quite well.

God has a way of breaking in. While I was trying to urge the prayer meeting on, others were protesting that we would get nowhere until we had fully, publicly and corporately repented before the Lord. I hadn't been trained to lead a prayer meeting in corporate repentance! What do you do? As I knelt at the front, I suggested that we turned to Revelation 3:14 onwards and quietly read the letter through. Then, in my own words, but based on that passage, I led the church together in an act and prayer of repentance. We had said it, meant and done it. But there was more to be done. We still needed to establish in the same public and corporate way the reality that Jesus was the head of his church, and the Spirit simply led us in what followed. I invited my colleagues on the staff team, and the church wardens who were present, to join me at the Holy Communion table and we held an impromptu induction service. I, as vicar, resigned as head, and put Christ into that position.

At that moment I was unable to continue. One of my wardens led us in prayer while I quietly cried for joy. We moved all around the church, to every significant place – pulpit, lectern, chancel steps, organ, choir stalls, pews, entrances – and at every point we asked Jesus to come into the midst and stay with us and be Lord and head of his church (the true and original meaning of Rev 3:20!).

We have never had any doubt that Jesus answered that prayer and came in. He began to do things and work his work among us. It was just a few months before the church's next Annual Meeting, and as I prepared for it I looked back to my address a year earlier and those guidelines I had spelt out. I discovered that as we made Jesus the Lord, so he was beginning to work things out for us.

The apparent simplicity of this turning point must not hide two important truths. First, a number of us were to experience depths of anguish, inner struggles, heated arguments and icy relationships from time to time. Second, we are continuing to work out year by year all that having Jesus as Lord means. I am not writing to share a 'success' story with you, but rather to give testimony to the utter faithfulness of the Lord to some of us who have been very slow to learn, and to pass on what he has been teaching us.

For me, these ground rules are just as relevant for churches in the shanty towns of Latin America or the villages of India as they are for us in outer London. They are as relevant and applicable to the senior leadership of the churches as they are to the newest clergy and ministers they may have ordained. What I write is relevant not only to church ministers and lay leaders but is true also for every church member who wishes to share completely in the life and work of his own local church.

What follows in *He is Lord* is the biblical evidence for and practical illustration of these guidelines. The book is an exposition of the lordship of Jesus for the local church corporately and for the individual Christian personally. Jesus has shown us again and again that if his lordship over the local church is to have any real meaning it must not be an experience in a particular week of prayer to which we look back, but a constant, daily reality within each section of the church, and for every member of the church. So we have been led on to discover what the lordship of Jesus means in the world of work and in the use of money and time, both for the members of the congregation and for the leadership gathered in worship and council, in devotion and decision.

It is essential to lay the firm biblical and theological foundation that Jesus is Lord before demonstrating what this means in practice. I therefore begin with this firm foundation, before moving on in Part One to relate this to the local church, and in Part Two to relate it very briefly to the individual Christian. The book ends with a short epilogue which will give us confidence in the Lord for the future, just as we have found security in him for the past.

The more I reflect upon the theme, the more I sense my own inability to write in a way that will honour the Lord. Yet I have been aware of his leading as I have written in the midst of a full parish life. The fact is, we won't truly understand and marvel at the lordship of Jesus and his amazing glory and grace until we see him face to face. But when that happens I won't need to write!

If I am asked what is the greatest need of the church throughout the world today, I would answer without doubt that it is to realise afresh the meaning of the lordship of Jesus for his church. The greatest need is not more exciting worship, more faithful giving, more dedicated leadership, more missionary zeal, more evangelistic outreach, better theological training, greater schemes for church unity or more social compassion. All these are needed and will result when the church throughout the world realises afresh that 'God exalted [Jesus] to the highest place and gave him the name that is above every name, that at the name of Jesus every knee should bow, in heaven and on earth and under the earth, and every tongue confess that Jesus Christ is Lord, to the glory of God the Father' (Phil 2:9–11).

# PART ONE

# 1 JESUS CHRIST IS LORD

I love London. One of my unfulfilled dreams is to have enough time, money and energy to explore its buildings, courts, history and tradition, to get to know the internal workings of its institutions and to understand the international influence London has.

The visitor to London will make sure he sees such historic sites as Westminster Abbey, the Houses of Parliament, Buckingham Palace and St Paul's Cathedral.

In our home we have a number of paintings of St Paul's. My favourite one hangs in my study. It depicts the Cathedral towering over the River Thames, the Law Courts, and government offices. In the background rise tall, modern buildings, but none can dwarf Sir Christopher Wren's proud and dominant Cathedral. The picture is a parable. God intends that he should govern and be Lord over all human institutions and powers, whether it be government, the law, the financial institutions, or the church.

Come with me inside the Cathedral and we shall find a different story. I wonder what would catch your eye. Is it the sense of God's presence and peace, other visitors, someone taking a photograph, the bookstall, the many inscriptions, the Whispering Gallery set high in the vaulted dome; is it the High Altar, the marbled floor, the vergers preparing the next worship service? Come with me in your imagination to one pillar on the south aisle of the Cathedral where there hangs another picture that tells a powerful story.

It is the picture entitled *The Light of the World*. The original of Holman Hunt's picture, painted in 1853, now hangs in Keble College, Oxford. The replica that we see in St Paul's was painted forty years after the original by the pre-Raphaelite artist. Writing to *The Times* on 5 May 1854, John Ruskin described the picture:

On the left-hand side of the picture is seen this door of the human soul. It is fast barred; its bars and nails are rusty; it is knitted and bound to its stanchions by creeping tendrils of ivy, showing that it has never been opened. A bat hovers about it; its threshold is overgrown with brambles, nettles and fruitless corn ... Christ approaches it in the night-time ...[1]

Jesus Christ as the Lord of his church is coming to claim his rightful place.

Just as the *picture* of Christ, *The Light of the World*, has been placed to one side of the Cathedral, so the *person* of Jesus as Lord of his church has been pushed to one side by many in his church at the present time. I have already shared with you in the preface how God used that same picture and passage of scripture (Rev 3:14–22) – the message of the risen Christ to the church at Laodicea (and Laodicea literally means 'man's ruling') – to convict one local church that Jesus Christ is Lord, asking that he might have his church back.

Some churches and fellowships are governed by the past and its traditions and others by neophilia – the latest craze; they may also be controlled by the position and power of their leaders – whether they be pope, archbishop, local minister, elder or lay leader.

Yet the confession of the early church is the simple affirmation, 'Jesus is Lord'. As St Paul puts it, writing to the church at Philippi:

Therefore God exalted him to the highest place and gave him the name that is above every name, that at the name of Jesus every knee should bow, in heaven and on earth and under the earth, and every tongue confess that Jesus Christ is Lord, to the glory of God the Father.

(Phil 2:9–11)

On what grounds did the early church believe and confess that Jesus is Lord, and why should the church at the end of the twentieth century make the same profession? I want to summon five major witnesses to give evidence of the lordship of Jesus:

i. The teaching of the New Testament
ii. The titles and names given to Jesus himself
iii. The major themes of the Old Testament
iv. The testimony of the Father and the Spirit
v. The task and witness of the Prophets.

The easiest place to begin is with the teaching of the New Testament.


## The teaching of the New Testament

Writing to the church at Ephesus, Paul tries to describe the power of the resurrection in these terms:

> That power is like the working of his mighty strength, which he exerted in Christ when he raised him from the dead and seated him at his right hand in the heavenly realms, far above all rule and authority, power and dominion, and every title that can be given, not only in the present age but also in the one to come. And God placed all things under his feet and appointed him to be head over everything for the church, which is his body, the fulness of him who fills everything in every way.
>
> (Eph 1:19–23)

A similar theme comes when Paul writes to the church at Colosse:

> He is the image of the invisible God, the firstborn over all creation. For by him all things were created: things in heaven and on earth, visible and invisible, whether thrones or powers or rulers or authorities; all things were created by him and for him. He is before all things, and in him all things hold together. And he is the head of the body, the church; he is the beginning and the firstborn

from among the dead, so that in everything he might
have the supremacy.

(Col 1:15–18)

On what grounds, therefore, does St Paul proclaim that
Jesus is Lord and head of the church? On the basis of what
Paul says in Colossians we can give three reasons. First,
Jesus has this right *because he is the revelation of God the
Father*. 'He is the image of the invisible God' (v.15) and
'God was pleased to have all his fulness dwell in him' (v.19).
While men are forbidden to make graven images of God,
Jesus perfectly reveals and reflects the image of the Father.
The same claim is made in John's gospel: 'In the beginning
was the Word, and the Word was with God, and the Word
was God. He was with God in the beginning . . . No-one
has ever seen God, but the only Son, who is at the Father's
side, has made him known' (John 1:1–2,18 mg.).

Second, Jesus has the right to be the head and Lord of his
church *because of the redemption he has obtained*. It is
through Christ that God reconciles all things to himself,
'whether things on earth or things in heaven, by making
peace through his blood, shed on the cross' (v.20). Through
his death upon the cross Jesus was to vanquish sin, defeat
Satan and destroy his power (Col 2:14–15). He sets us free
from the fear of death, which can hold people in bondage
all their lives (Heb 2:15), and his resurrection declares and
demonstrates that he is the Son of God (Rom 1:4).

Third, Jesus is head of his church *because this is the
relationship and honour he has been given by the Father*
(v.18), and indeed he has that sovereign relationship, not
only with his church but also with the whole of creation, by
virtue of God's plan and purpose.

Jesus is not the founder of a world religion because he is a
perfect man. He is the author and finisher of the faith and
Lord of the church because he is the incarnate Son of God
who died on the cross and rose again from the tomb. Such a
testimony is the consistent theme of the New Testament
(Eph 1:19–23; 4:14–16; Phil 2:5–11; Col 1:15–18; Heb
1:1–3).

## The titles and names given to Jesus himself

Here is the second witness to establish our claim that Jesus is Lord. The claim that Jesus makes more frequently than any other in his teaching is 'I am' – I am the bread of life (Jn 6:35), the light of the world (Jn 8:12), the way, the truth and the life (Jn 14:6), the resurrection and the life (Jn 11:25), the good shepherd (Jn 10:11), the true vine (Jn 15:1), etc. As he makes these claims, so he takes to himself the very name of almighty God.

When God called Moses to lead his people out of Egypt to the promised land, and Moses asked what was God's name, God replied 'I AM WHO I AM. This is what you are to say to the Israelites: I AM has sent me to you' (Exod 3:14). Jesus takes that divine name and applies it to himself. In the very last chapter of the book of Revelation, Jesus is spoken of as 'the Alpha and the Omega, the First and the Last, the Beginning and the End . . . the Root and the Offspring of David, and the bright Morning Star' (Rev 22:13,16).

An exhaustive study of the Bible will reveal that Jesus was given more than one hundred and fifty different names and titles as the second person of the Trinity. Admittedly some are obscure, but among the main names not already mentioned are the following: The last or second Adam (1 Cor 15:45); the Ancient of Days (Dan 7:22); the author and perfecter of our faith (Heb 12:2); the author of our salvation (Heb 2:10); the cornerstone (Eph 2:20 and 1 Peter 2:6); the Creator (Isa 40:28); the Everlasting Father (Isa 9:6); the heir of all things (Heb 1:2); the apostle and high priest (Heb 3:1); Immanuel – God with us (Isa 7:14; Mt 1:23); the King of kings and Lord of lords (1 Tim 6:15; Rev 19:16); the Anointed One – or the Messiah (Dan 9:25), and the one who is the same yesterday, today and for ever (Heb 13:8).

In addition to the titles that were bestowed upon Jesus, there is 'The name that is above every name' (Phil 2:9) that is given to him. Jesus' position as Lord is established by both his nature – who he is – and also his name – the power and authority he possesses.

It was Charles Haddon Spurgeon who told the story of visiting a woman, now in her old age and poverty, who had once been a maid to a wealthy woman. He noticed that upon the wall of the dimly lit room in which the old lady lay was framed a faded document. Asking if he might look more closely at 'the picture', Spurgeon discovered that he was holding in his hands a substantial bequest given to the woman by her former mistress. The old lady didn't understand her right to be able to act on the bequest which she had possessed for some time. Had she done so it would have dramatically transformed the humble and poor surrounding in which she was spending her dying days.

The church is in danger of doing the same thing unless it discovers not only that Jesus is Lord but also that the Lord bestows upon his church the power of his name (i.e. something to transform our day by day existence):

> He has bestowed upon Him honour, and glory and power, and seated Him at His own right hand in the heavenlies, far above every known authority; and now, all this honour, this glory, this authority, this power, is vested in the Name of Jesus, and this Name is given to us.[2]

It was because they acknowledged the name of Jesus, that the members of the early church powerfully proclaimed the message of salvation, effectively gave themselves to the service of their Lord, regularly entered into prayer and supplication, and willingly faced persecution and suffering.

Every generation of Christians and churches needs to discover and acknowledge that Jesus is Lord. In his book *How Do Churches Grow?* Roy Pointer of the Bible Society states that the starting point in how to get a church ready for growth is to acknowledge the headship of Jesus.

> Therefore the first step for any local church that wants to grow is a conscious acknowledgement by all that Jesus Christ is Lord and Head. Every church must want the will of Christ to direct its affairs and the Spirit of Christ to

empower its activities. This united confession and desire is essential for genuine growth.[3]

One such church whose testimony would bear this out is Gold Hill Baptist Church in Buckinghamshire, England. Writing in *Renewal* magazine, their senior pastor, Jim Graham, tells of a memorable weekend houseparty at Hildenborough Hall when

> God the Holy Spirit came among us and upon us corporately . . . The first evidence of God at work among us in this remarkable way was not ecstatic worship (that came later!) but a gentle and simple repentance that occurred at a depth of fellowship that I have never known previously.[4]

Again and again I find that God is calling his church to repentance as the first response to the lordship of Jesus. It is here that new things begin in a church. Reflecting on that remarkable weekend, Jim Graham writes further: 'There was the unshakeable commitment to the reality that Jesus is who he claimed to be – "the Messiah, the Son of the living God". With that secured, Jesus now was released to fulfil the main purpose of his mission . . .'

## The major themes of the Old Testament

We must never forget that our Christian faith is based on the revelation of both the New and the Old Testaments, and centres upon the three persons of the Trinity, not just upon Jesus of Nazareth. Thus, while we can establish the lordship of Jesus over his church upon the nature and the names of Jesus revealed in the New Testament, we have a still fuller and firmer base if we take other evidence into account. For example, we have the major themes of the Old Testament as a powerful demonstration of the lordship of Jesus.

Walking back to the village of Emmaus from the city of

Jerusalem on the first Easter Sunday evening, the risen Lord fell into conversation with two confused and distraught disciples who could not understand all that had happened during the last few days. Their master, Jesus of Nazareth, had been crucified. He had taught them that he would suffer and be killed and on the third day would rise from the dead, but as far as they knew, no resurrection had occurred and all their hopes had been in vain. Jesus had to rebuke the two disciples for being slow to believe all that the prophets had spoken: 'Did not the Christ have to suffer these things and then enter his glory? And beginning with Moses and all the Prophets, he explained to them what was said in all the Scriptures concerning himself' (Lk 24:26–27).

In other words, Jesus is teaching that his lordship which is revealed in the New Testament is concealed in the Old Testament.

It would require a whole book to deal fully with such a marvellous subject as Christ in all the Scriptures,[5] but consider the following topics from the Old Testament that reveal and reflect the lordship of Jesus.

## The covenant

The Bible begins with creation, and we have already noted that Jesus is the author and sustainer of creation. It is also true that the theme of the covenant is a glorious biblical truth, and Christ's lordship is seen in both creation and covenant.[6]

The covenant is a divine, sovereign and unilateral declaration of God's grace towards people. Throughout the Old Testament God is revealing his covenant plans and purposes, first through Noah, and then Abraham, Moses and David.

God speaks of 'the book of the Covenant' that contained the commandments, 'the ark of the covenant' that symbolised his presence, and the blood of the covenant that foreshadowed the one perfect sacrifice of Christ. 'Each covenant grows progressively richer in promises, until the coming of Christ ushers in the "new covenant".'[7] Christ ushers in the new covenant, sealing it with his shed blood. There are not two different and contradictory covenants. The new doesn't terminate or contradict the old, but rather fulfils it in Christ. As John puts it, 'From the fulness of his grace we have all received one blessing after another. For the law was given through Moses; grace and truth came through Jesus Christ' (Jn 1:16–17).

## The one perfect sacrifice

The covenant of God expresses the relationship he desires to have with us, a relationship that requires obedience and holiness. Sin has marred that relationship and requires that atonement – or 'At-one-ment' – should be made.

God decreed under the old covenant that such atonement would be brought about by sacrifice. The Old Testament sacrifices such as the sin and guilt offerings and supremely the sacrifices offered on the annual Day of Atonement (Lev 16) foreshadowed the perfect sacrifice of Christ.

Sacrifices in the Old Testament spoke – in their variety – of both fellowship with God and feasting in his presence on the one hand, and of receiving forgiveness and discovering freedom from sin on the other. However, these Old Testament sacrifices could never take away sin. Thus, the writer to the Hebrews contrasting the old and the new covenants, and expressing the continuity that the new had with the old, states:

> Day after day every priest stands and performs his religious duties; again and again he offers the same sacrifices, which can never take away sins. But when this priest had offered for all time one sacrifice for sins, he sat down at the right hand of God . . . because by one sacrifice he has made perfect for ever those who are being made holy.
>
> (Heb 10:11–14)

## The Lamb of God

The biblical image that most clearly portrays sacrifice and declares the sovereignty of Jesus is the theme of the Lamb of God. The lamb was foreshadowed in the offering of Isaac by Abraham (Gen 22:7–8,13–14), eaten at Passover (Exod 12:3–5), offered up in Leviticus (Lev 12:6), prophesied by Isaiah (Isa 53:7), preached about by John the Baptist (Jn 1:29,36), fulfilled by the Lord Jesus Christ (1 Cor 5:7), taught by Philip (Acts 8:32–35), explained by Peter (1 Pet 1:18–19), and worshipped in adoration and triumph by the church in glory (Rev 5:6,8,12–13).

In the same way that the covenant and sacrifice reveal and reflect the lordship of Jesus, so also do other themes such as the tabernacle, the great high priest, the redeemer, and Christ as the fulfilling of the law. Two other Old Testament themes also clearly illustrate the lordship of Jesus: Christ as the Servant-Messiah, and as the Shepherd-King.


## The Servant-Messiah

The strange truth about the Messiah is that the word is used so rarely in the Bible. It is used twice in the Old Testament in Daniel 9:25–26 and is found in the New Testament as the Greek word 'Christ'. Both words – Christ and Messiah – mean 'the Anointed One of God'.

The Old Testament is like a treasure hunt, disclosing over many centuries different clues about God's chosen and anointed servant who is fully and finally revealed only in the person of Jesus. The Festival of Nine Lessons and Carols loved by so many throughout the world at Christmas-time illustrates just this theme. No one group of people has done more than the choir and musicians of King's College, Cambridge, to share with millions around the world these familiar words: 'Therefore let us read and mark in Holy Scripture the tale of the loving purposes of God from the first days of our disobedience unto the glorious redemption brought us by this Holy

Child: and let us make this place glad with our carols of praise.'[8]

As the promises from Genesis 3:15 to Isaiah 7:14,9:2, 6–7; 11:1ff; Micah 5:2–4; Zechariah 9:9 are read, the coming of the Messiah who would set his people free is foretold. He would be God's Son, born of a virgin; he would bring the blessings of God's rule and light, be the bringer of peace, and would be the foundation stone upon which people would build their lives. But the Messiah would be the servant who would also suffer.

There is no fuller description of Christ's suffering on the cross than Isaiah 53 in the Old Testament, and no clearer identification that this is Jesus than in Acts 8:26–40.

Philip the evangelist, beginning with Isaiah 53, told the Ethiopian Chancellor of the Exchequer the good news about Jesus. At once the Ethiopian declares his faith that Jesus is Lord and is baptised. Such a revelation was too startling and contrary to traditional expectations for many Jews to accept. It was a truth that would cause God's people to stumble and fall.

## The Shepherd-King

The Bible is an eastern book, and the shepherd is a very familiar figure. It was the shepherd who both cared for the sheep and ruled over the people. Sadly, Israel's human leaders and shepherds were false and needed to be rebuked by God. But God said that he himself would be the shepherd of his people (Ps 23:1; 80:1; 100:3; Isa 40:11). What is said in the Old Testament about God as the shepherd of his people is fulfilled by Jesus in the New. Indeed, the New Testament reveals Jesus as 'the good shepherd' who lays down his life for the sheep, as 'the great shepherd' who is brought back from the dead, and as 'the Chief Shepherd' who will come again one day and reward his servants (Jn 10:11–16; Heb 13:20; 1 Pet 5:4).

So, once again, we see demonstrated the lordship of Jesus in these majestic and glorious themes concealed in the Old but revealed in the New. There is one other way in which the lordship of Jesus is demonstrated. To the Jews their great heroes and leaders were men like Abraham, Jacob, Elijah, David, Solomon, Jonah, and even John the Baptist, but the consistent testimony is that Christ is greater than each one of these (Mt 11:11; 12:41–42; 22:43–45; Mk 9:3–8; Jn 4:12; 8:53).

We have invited three dependable witnesses (the New Testament's teaching, Jesus' titles, the Old Testament themes) to testify to the lordship of Jesus. Jesus himself was once challenged on this very issue. In John 5 we read of the healing of the man who had lain at the pool of Bethesda as an invalid for thirty-eight years. Jesus heals the man at once and calls him to pick up his mat and walk.

Unfortunately the Jews did not react kindly to the fact that Jesus had healed the man on the sabbath day! Jesus was drawn headlong into a conflict about his authority and position. You will find – if you read the account from verse 16 onwards – that Jesus summons various witnesses. Among them are the works he did, and the testimony of the scriptures. We have addressed ourselves to these. He called two other witnesses – his Father, and John the Baptist. To these we must turn, if only briefly.

## The testimony of the Father and the Spirit

I rejoice that the Christian faith is a trinitarian faith – based upon God the Father, the Son and the Holy Spirit. I find that it makes sense of the biblical record. Every major doctrine is established upon this firm trinitarian foundation. God the Father depends upon Jesus the Son, and Jesus depends upon the Father. While Jesus could only do what he saw the Father doing, the Father was equally dependent upon the Son to make the Father known. Likewise the Lord Jesus together with the Father is the one who bestows upon his church the Holy Spirit, and the work of the Holy Spirit is to help people understand more of the person and work of Jesus. As Jesus put it:

I have much more to say to you, more than you can now bear. But when he, the Spirit of truth, comes, he will guide you into all truth. He will not speak on his own: he will speak only what he hears, and he will tell you what is yet to come. He will bring glory to me by taking what is mine and making it known to you.

(Jn 16:12–14)

The Holy Spirit is the self-effacing person of the Godhead, turning people's gaze back to Jesus, and Jesus is the one who reveals and reflects the Father. Thus the Spirit points the way to Jesus as Lord and God. No wonder that Thomas, after the resurrection and a period of real, personal doubt, fell down on his knees before Jesus of Nazareth and proclaimed, 'My Lord and my God!' (Jn 20:28).

## The task and witness of the prophets

I love John Eddison's description of John the Baptist as the patron saint of silver medallists.[9] John constantly pointed away to Jesus. Christ had to be first, and he had to put himself in the background, yet John found complete fulfilment in acknowledging the lordship of Jesus. John described himself as a voice or a herald announcing the coming of the King. His ministry was to prepare the way of the Lord. He pointed the way to Jesus as the Lamb of God who takes away the sin of the world, and as the one who would baptise people with the Holy Spirit (Jn 1:29,33). Now, only the perfect Son of God could be the sin-bearer and saviour, and only the Messiah, the one who was himself anointed with the Holy Spirit and power, would be able to bestow the Holy Spirit upon others. John described himself as the friend of the bridegroom, and Jesus as the bridegroom waiting for his bride, the church. No wonder John's message is summed up in these words: 'He must become greater; I must become less' (Jn 3:30).

## The lordship of Jesus today

From beginning to end, the Bible demonstrates that Jesus is Lord. Genesis begins with God saying, 'Let us make . . .' (Gen 1:26), and there we have the simplest expression of the three persons of the Godhead active in creation. There is Jesus in his pre-incarnate existence with God. The last pages of the Bible speak of the coming again of Jesus in the same terms that would be applied to the Father (Rev 22:12–16). In between we have the irrefutable testimony that Jesus is Lord. The Old Testament in its major themes proclaims this. John the Baptist as the last of the prophets continues and completes the prophetic function to point a way to Jesus and prepare people for his coming. The Father and the Spirit, within the fellowship of the Godhead, point a way to Jesus as equal with them in the Trinity and each dependent upon the other. The New Testament records the works and ministry of Jesus, culminating in his death and resurrection, thus proclaiming that Jesus is Lord. The early Church joined in that confession and the church down the years has maintained that witness.

Yet there is still the need for the church of the present generation to join in that same triumphal profession and proclaim and confess that Jesus is Lord. It is our urgent and great need to establish in practice and work out in detail the lordship of Jesus.

A leading and outstanding Christian missionary society asked its officers and committee members to work out what they felt were the urgent priorities before the church in Britain at the end of the 1980s. A great variety of different answers were given. For example, among the first ten, the following priorities were given: training lay people to share their faith; tackling the urban and inner-city areas; reaching men; strengthening family life; planting new churches; responding to change. They are all important priorities, and until a few years ago would have reflected my own personal list. But I have to admit that the first priority on my present list was not even in the first ten of the overall list.

*I firmly believe that the greatest need of the church in*

*Britain – and possibly throughout the world – is to acknowl-
edge that Jesus is the Lord, that he is the head of the church
and Lord of every member, and then to work that out in
practice day by day.*

Again and again the message that the risen Christ speaks
to his church today is that 'he wants his church back'. He
longs to be restored to his rightful place as its Lord and its
head.

Some of us have only just begun to work this out. We are
still working at it, and I anticipate we will do so until we die.
Having laid the biblical foundations, the rest of the book
will seek to do two things. First, to work out what the
lordship of Jesus means for the corporate church – and that
can be revolutionary – and, second, to spell out for every
individual church member what it means to acknowledge
Jesus as Lord. His lordship is challenging and yet liberating, for 'if the Son sets you free, you will be free indeed' and
'where the Spirit of the Lord is, there is freedom' (Jn 8:36;
2 Cor 3:17).

# For personal reflection or group study

1 Would you agree that the greatest need of your local church or
fellowship is to recognise Jesus as the Lord and head of his
church?

2 We live in a multifaith and multiracial society. Are Christians
right – or arrogant – to claim that Jesus is Lord and God? What
arguments set out in this chapter would you use to support your
argument?

3 If you haven't already done so, look up the biblical references
to one of the following themes:

○ Christ as the head of the church (p. 19–20)
○ Christ as the Lamb of God (p. 26)
○ Christ as the one who is greater (p. 28)

How might they help you support the claims of Christ in a
discussion with a nominal churchgoer, a Jew or a member of
another faith?

# 2 WORSHIP THE LORD

Worship is the only adequate response to the lordship of Jesus. For example, Jesus said to Thomas, 'Put your finger here; see my hands. Reach out your hand and put it into my side. Stop doubting and believe.' Thomas answered, 'My Lord and my God!' (Jn 20:27–28). Or again: 'Then the eleven disciples went to Galilee, to the mountain where Jesus had told them to go. When they saw him, they worshipped him . . .' (Mt 28:16–17).

There is no topic guaranteed to stir up more tension and argument in the life of a local church than what we call worship. Change a hymn tune, introduce new music, amend the order of service, move the church furniture around, and in many congregations there will be trouble. Yet there is no experience in the Christian life that can be more powerful and liberating than true worship. My purpose in this chapter is, therefore, to illustrate how the acknowledgement that Jesus is Lord will radically and positively affect our worship. My aim is not to cover the essential theme of worship itself. There are other helpful books which have already done this.[1] Once Jesus has been established as Lord of a congregation – or even of an individual Christian – our worship will be affected in at least five different ways.


## The meaning and extent of worship

A first way in which the lordship of Jesus will affect our worship is in our understanding of what worship really is. We shall stop defining worship in terms of a specific act of worship in a consecrated building on a Sunday, and see that worship relates to our lives from Monday to Saturday as well.

We are told to worship in spirit and in truth, and we are taught to walk in the Spirit, and to walk in the light and truth of God. Thus the true division in life is not between Sunday and Monday, but between the flesh and the Spirit. We can work and live in the flesh, and we can also worship in the flesh – i.e. self governs when we go to church, what type of service we go to, etc. – but we are to worship in the Spirit and to work in the Spirit.

Bishop Michael Marshall likens worship to the whole way of seeing God's world from God's point of view in Christ.[2] Graham Kendrick says that worship is 'celebrating the truth about God' and so all life is celebrating the truth about God, for he is concerned with the whole of life.[3] William Temple also makes the same point when writing about the Christian citizen:

> If then the Christian citizen is to make his Christianity tell upon his politics, his business and his social enterprises, he must be a churchman – consciously belonging to the worshipping fellowship and sharing its worship before he is a citizen. He must bring the concerns of his citizenship and his business before God and go forth to them carrying God's inspiration with him.[4]

St Paul makes the same appeal in Romans 12:1–2:

> Therefore, I urge you, brothers, in view of God's mercy, to offer your bodies as living sacrifices, holy and pleasing to God – this is your spiritual act of worship. Do not conform any longer to the pattern of this world, but be transformed by the renewing of your mind. Then you will be able to test and approve what God's will is – his good, pleasing and perfect Will.

(We may note in passing that worship should affect our bodies.)

All I want to stress at this point is that when Jesus becomes Lord of his church and of its members then worship is not an activity lasting an hour or two each week, but is an attitude towards every hour of each week, because Jesus is Lord of time and eternity.

## The importance of worship

Secondly, worship will be given its rightful place. It will be the first priority in our life and thinking. This has not always been so. For some, evangelism or mission was the priority. For others it was the pursuit of social issues and the changing of social structures and conditions in which people live. For Christians who have made Jesus Lord in South Africa or in the areas of racial tension in America, the first response is worship from which a lasting change in black–white relationships can come about. For Christians imprisoned for their faith in Russian labour camps the first response is worship. For believers eking out an existence in the favellas (or shanty towns) of South America the prime concern is not better housing, but their love and worship of the Lord.

Writing to the Jewish Christians who had been forced to leave home and flee from persecution because of their new-found faith, Peter reminds them that they are 'a chosen people, a royal priesthood, a holy nation, a people belonging to God, that [they] may declare the praises of [God] who called [them] out of darkness into his wonderful light. Once [they] were not a people, but now [they] are the people of God; once [they] had not received mercy, but now [they] have received mercy' (1 Pet 2:9–10).

The apostle Paul makes the same point when he writes to the church at Ephesus. Those Christians lived in a world of lax moral behaviour, subtle social pressures and heated battles over trade disputes – and yet Paul reminds them that God has chosen them in Christ 'before the creation of the world to be holy and blameless in his sight . . . to the praise of his glorious grace' (Eph 1:4–6).

Worship is not only to be our first response to the lordship of Jesus, it is the foundation supporting the whole of the Christian life. It is the principal activity of the saints and the elders in heaven, and it is the object of Satan's attack here on earth from start to finish (Rev 4:9–11; 5:14; 7:11; Mt 4:9–10, cf. Gen 3:1–4).

A. W. Tozer once described worship as 'the missing jewel of the Evangelical Church'. Worship should have the first place because of what it is and what it results in. Worship expresses our relationship and response to God. It has been described as 'loving God in the presence of one another, and loving one another in the presence of God'.[5] This fulfils *the great commandment* that Jesus gave that we should love the Lord our God with all our heart, soul, strength and mind, and our neighbour as ourselves (Mt 22:34–40; Mk 12:28–34; Lk 10:25–28).

*The great commission* also grew out of worship. It was after the disciples had worshipped the risen Lord, and were made aware of his authority and power that Jesus gave them the commission to 'go and make disciples of all nations, baptising them in the name of the Father and of the Son and of the Holy Spirit, and teaching them to obey everything I have commanded you. And surely I am with you always, to the very end of the age' (Mt 28:16–20).

Significant developments in the missionary programme of the church sprang from worship. For example, when the early church at Antioch was seeking the leading of God we read: 'While they were worshipping the Lord and fasting, the Holy Spirit said, "Set apart for me Barnabas and Saul for the work to which I have called them"' (Acts 13:2).

When the church in Macedonia was facing great financial need, and longed to give effectively, 'they gave themselves first to the Lord and then to us in keeping with God's will' (2 Cor 8:5). The secret of effective giving was found in worship.

The word used in Acts 13:2 for worship is *Leiturgeo* – from which we derive the word 'liturgy', which means to equip. It was the word used to describe the way that a loyal Greek subject would give money to equip a naval unit or to help train a choir.[6] Worship has the effect of equipping us for the work of the Lord.

## Guidelines for worship

Thirdly, our worship of Jesus as Lord will be governed by
God-given principles rather than by human preference or
man-made traditions. Worship will be seen as something
that is Christ-pleasing, not man-centred.

### *Worship is commanded by God, and a personal response to God himself*

'Worship is not the singing of hymns or the reading of
prayers. Worship is the offering of your own life to the Lord
in response to him and without that you have not
worshipped.'[7] Graham Kendrick has written that worship
is not optional, but is commanded in both the Old and the
New Testament: 'there are commands to praise, glorify,
sing praises, shout, bless, give thanks, bow down, kneel
before, offer, sing a new song to, rejoice, honour, offer
sacrifices, exalt, fear, adore, serve, extol, magnify and
many others too'.[8] William Temple, also, has given us this
beautiful definition of worship: 'To worship is to quicken
the conscience by the holiness of God, to feed the mind
with the truth of God, to purge the imagination by the
beauty of God, to open the heart to the love of God, and to
devote the will to the purposes of God.'[9] Just as a husband
is commanded to love his wife as Christ loves us, but in
practice responds to his wife not out of obedience, but from
a willing heart, so our worship of God is commanded, and
yet is the ready response from those who truly know the
Lord. Worship thus becomes something that is dynamic. It
will be alive, beautiful and satisfying rather than being dull,
routine and boring. Worship will be both timeless and
timely.

### *The elements of worship will be changeless because God is changeless*

We will still need to praise God and bring our confession
to him. We shall find a place for both petition and

intercession, for praise and penitence, for listening and thanksgiving, for adoration and supplication. The Lord does not change and thus the elements that make up worship should not change.

## The ways in which we express worship's unchanging elements will change

This is because habits, customs and culture will change from place to place and year to year. Sadly, some churches wish to continue worshipping God with sixteenth-century English (the AV) and eighteenth-century hymns and nineteenth-century ways (chanting) in thirteenth-century buildings. The trappings and externals have become the all-important considerations – no wonder some people find no reality in their worship. As Eddie Gibbs has perceptively asked: 'If you didn't have to go to your church, would you?';[10] or as Graham Kendrick has written: 'If a sincere and honest stranger was invited to an average Christian meeting . . . would he feel that he was attending a memorial service for a God who is dead, or a celebration of a rich and abundant life poured out by a God who is alive?'[11]

## True worshippers

Questions about the externals of worship are not new. Jesus encountered them when he spoke with the woman at Jacob's well. As a Samaritan, she would have been taught that Mount Gerizim was the place appointed for the offering of sacrifice and worship. Hence her comment to Jesus: 'Our fathers worshipped on this mountain, but you Jews claim that the place where we must worship is in Jerusalem.' Jesus went on to explain to her the fundamental truths about worship:

Believe me, woman, a time is coming when you will worship the Father neither on this mountain nor in Jerusalem. You Samaritans worship what you do not know; we worship what we do know, for salvation is from the Jews. Yet a time is coming and has now come when the true worshippers will worship the Father in spirit and truth, for they are the kind of worshippers the Father seeks. God is spirit, and his worshippers must worship in spirit and in truth.

(Jn 4:20–24)

There are three essential truths about worship in this passage.

*We must know the Father.* To know God means that we know God in personal experience, as a husband and wife know each other, rather than knowing *about* God – just as I know Mount Everest is over 29,000 ft, but I have never climbed it. When Paul was in Athens (Acts 17:22–23) he saw that in every way the people there were very religious. As he walked round the city and observed their objects of worship, he found an altar with this inscription: TO AN UNKNOWN GOD. 'Now what you worship as something unknown I am going to proclaim to you,' was Paul's reaction. We know God through Jesus Christ, whom the Father has sent (Jn 17:3). We know God as we find that Jesus is the way to God, the truth about God and the life of God (Jn 14:6). The problems some people have with worship are not centred upon the externals of worship, but in their own hearts (as with the woman at the well). They do not yet know the God whom they are trying to worship.

*Worship is made alive and real through the Spirit.* We are to worship in spirit, says Jesus. There are two confessions that the Spirit enables every Christian to make. First, we cry *Abba*, Father (Rom 8:15) and know God as Father and ourselves as children of God. Second, we confess that 'Jesus is Lord' (1 Cor 12:3). Thus the more fully we confess the lordship of Christ, so the greater will be the reality of the Spirit's ministry in our worship. Just as the Spirit of God came and touched the dryness of the bones in Ezekiel's vision and made them live (Ezek 37:9–10), so the Holy Spirit can touch the dryness of our worship and make that live.

Perhaps I can illustrate this truth from our church's own experience. For more than two years we have called our ministry team and others to pray together before the evening service. Let me explain our pattern of worship which, although it is an Anglican one, illustrates a truth for every church, whatever its background. On three Sundays of the month we use the new liturgy of the *Alternative Service Book* (ASB), with modern hymns and songs, and on the fourth we have the traditional 1662 Prayer Book service, with chanting, anthems and canticles. For some of us in the ministry team this was a real barrier in worship. We were not convinced that God was able to use and work through such traditional liturgy, as he could the modern, and if we had had our way we would have dropped it completely and would have upset a part of our congregation very deeply.

God chose to do things differently. He began to change attitudes towards the older service, and towards those who preferred it. We had to repent of our unbelief that God couldn't work through something traditional, and we had to confess our lack of love and impatience with those who found this the service they preferred. Because we had these problems, we always found that we prayed 'harder' and confessed our problems to the Lord in the pre-service prayer time, and God in his grace always answered and seemed to bless people's lives more fully on that fourth Sunday than on the others. While God brought changes to the worship, he brought many more changes to the worshippers. The true dynamic in worship is the Holy Spirit of God. 'To worship "in spirit" is to tap into the very source of worship himself, the inexhaustible, endlessly praising Spirit of God, and to allow him liberty to join with our own spirit in expressing through our mind and body the worth of our saviour Jesus, and the love of our heavenly Father.'[12]

While our worship is to be in Spirit and in truth, there are also some very practical and down to earth implications that can cause worship to be either effective or unhelpful. One of these, for example, will be the need to ensure that churches are warm. You cannot easily worship if your teeth

are chattering and your feet are cold. Therefore it is right to
give attention to where we worship – whether in a school
hall, a home, or a church hall – if the church or chapel itself
is too expensive to heat. You need to be familiar with the
words and the music. We need to help the congregation
share fully in the worship, and so the giving out of page
numbers, and the preparation and presentation of the
service are important.

Again, to worship in Spirit does not mean that we are
slipshod and leave things to the last minute. It is just as
important to seek the guidance of the Spirit in selecting
hymns – even if it is done months ahead – or in praying over
preaching themes. There is great joy in discovering the
Lord's leading, when what was chosen two or three months
ahead was just right for a particular situation. For example,
we had chosen to preach through the minor prophets
during the mornings after Easter in a year when a General
Election was called, and we were due to have a pre-election
service with the candidates of all the main political parties
present. The subject was Haggai! Could there be a more
pertinent comment than this: 'Give careful thought to your
ways. You have planted much, but have harvested little.
You eat, but never have enough. You drink, but never have
your fill. You put on clothes, but are not warm. You earn
wages, only to put them in a purse with holes in it' (Hag
1:5–6). After the sermon, all the candidates thought the
preacher was going to vote for them, and Haggai was
described by a Cabinet Minister present as giving the best
definition of inflation he had known!

The Spirit can and will guide in planning in advance, in
final preparation and in the actual leading and sharing in
worship. He makes it real.

*Worship should be 'in truth'.* Our worship must express the
revealed truth we have about God himself. Let me give you
one illustration. In some places the worship is lofty and
exalted, and one is left with the feeling that God is very
remote and almost unknowable. In another fellowship, one
is given the impression that God is at our beck and call, and

we are on very 'matey' terms with the Almighty. Both situations are grave distortions of the truth. God is both very near and knowable, and also high and exalted, and our worship should express both.

Worship will develop and grow as we understand more about God himself. But the truth which fashions our worship is not only *revealed* truth, it will be truth to which we have *responded* – which we have allowed to clothe and fashion our lives. The more we do this, responding to the truth with our hearts as well as our heads, the more we shall discover 'reality' in our worship.

The apostle Paul sums up these principles when he writes to the Ephesians: 'Be filled with the Spirit. Speak to one another in psalms, hymns and spiritual songs. Sing and make music in your heart to the Lord, always giving thanks to God the Father for everything, in the name of our Lord Jesus Christ' (Eph 5:18–20).

The worship which is acceptable to God and satisfying to his people is worship by people who are allowing the Spirit to go on filling them moment by moment; worship that flows from a fellowship which has right relationships at its heart, whose members love one another and who know what it is to forgive one another as Christ forgave them. Acceptable worship flows from the heart, not just from the mouth and mind. Such worship will be the love song of the church towards her Lord, as a bride expressing her love towards her bridegroom.

Worship will become richer the more each person involved in it personally acknowledges Jesus as Lord – this is true for the congregation, preacher, minister and elders, priests and deacons, worship leader, organist and musicians, lesson readers, those who welcome or have any other part to play.

## Handling the problems in worship

The fourth aspect in which worship will be affected once we own the lordship of Jesus will be in the way we tackle the practical difficulties and tensions many people face in worship, whether they incline to a traditional, modern or charismatic view of worship. It is in the practical outworkings that the real problems arise.

The more traditional worshippers find it hard to accept modern worship songs and the seemingly endless repetition of simple words. Again, some of the congregation find it hard to have new songs and hymns introduced at every service – it seems as if the goodly heritage of Christian music has been rejected once and for all, never to be used again. Others find themselves threatened if they do not know what is going to happen next in the service, because they have found security in the familiar liturgical pattern. Others are very wary of anything that hints at emotion and are embarrassed by such activities as dance or drama, or even the introduction of banners. Again, it may be acceptable to genuflect and bow the head at the name of Jesus, but such action as raising hands and arms in worship just isn't done!

Many of us are so used to being passive spectators in worship, that when we are called upon to be active participants, allowing the whole of ourselves (mind, heart, body, spirit) to respond to the whole of God himself, we have problems. We are happy to go to church when we know that the sermon will last ten minutes and the service will be over in about an hour, but now it is so unpredictable and can go on and on. These are some of the difficulties that the more traditional worshipper faces.

Conversely, those who find a more open and less structured form of worship helpful face problems with a closely controlled time of worship which moves from one 'item' to the next. There is no 'space' when God can possibly get a look in and share anything with the congregation. There is no opportunity for the gifts of the Spirit to be expressed, and how can God really be worshipped in chanting when you don't know what to do, and can't even hear the words the choir is singing? Does not such worship quench the Spirit? After all, doesn't St Paul teach that 'the letter kills, but the Spirit gives life' (2 Cor 3:6)? These are real problems, and we must not lightly dismiss them. But we can also affirm that when Jesus is Lord there are practical solutions and ways forward.

For example, when Jesus is Lord of the church and her members, a new attitude of love towards each other will be expressed. Instead of shutting one another up in 'traditional' or 'renewal' or 'modern' boxes, and not allowing the two to meet, love will break down the barriers. Where the Spirit of the Lord is allowed to flow freely, he will take away fear, and bring love, power and self-control. There will be a growing together of the members, and an understanding and appreciation of each other. There will be an emphasis on building one another up, rather than insisting upon our own preferences. We shall begin to see that what matters most in worship is not whether a hymn or song or anthem pleases us, but whether it is acceptable and pleasing to God.

We shall find that when we make Jesus Lord he will begin to change our attitudes to the forms of service. Instead of some services being a hindrance and a barrier to us, we shall discover that God can and does use every form of worship that is 'in spirit and in truth'. He will show us a way to draw different traditions and styles of worship together, still keeping it so that the congregation feels secure with familiar words, but can then 'bridge' into a new item with the right song and music. We are learning more and more the value of 'bridging' or 'linking' one item to another, and in that way it is possible to hold together different traditions on special occasions.

It is possible for a traditional choir and a freer-style music group to grow together. They might become one group, they might have members common to both. Instead of battle lines being drawn up when people are seeking to defend their corner, a common allegiance and a growing love for each other stems from a central allegiance to Jesus, who becomes the bridge spanning both groups. As Andrew Maries writes: 'In Christ we are set free to enjoy and express the whole of life, not cut ourselves off in isolated corners, feeling threatened when invaded by something outside our normal experience. As whole people we are to embrace every experience and incorporate it into worship.'[13]

Teaching will play a vital part in reconciling different elements in worship. It is the unexplained change that is unnerving and difficult to grasp. Our congregations are made up of intelligent people. If they feel we respect them and are willing to spend time explaining changes before they happen, we are more likely to carry people with us, and they to move forward.

If we are willing to teach, we must also be willing to learn from others, but not simply to copy. We are all at different stages. What is right and works in church 'A', may be a disaster in church 'B'. The *Book of Common Prayer* was right for Britain in the nineteenth century, but it is not right for Africa in the twentieth – or even the twenty-first. The 'laid back' style of worship for four thousand people gathered in an old warehouse in California is not suitable for a small chapel or church in the South of England.

While the guidelines governing worship will be the same, the surroundings and settings will vary widely and we shall need to distinguish between what we do from principle and what we do as a result of our cultural heritage and conditioning.

We must also be patient and open when seeking to bring about changes in worship under Christ's lordship. Too many churches have to face the fact that 'we never did it this way before'! (The seven last words of a church?)

Early in 1986 we held a 'Music in Worship' weekend under the leadership of Robin Sheldon.[14] The purpose of the weekend was threefold:

i. To harmonise different musical traditions of the church and to have a unity of Spirit, while expressing a diversity in operation.
ii. To educate the congregation in the basic issues of music and worship.
iii. To excite and encourage the musical gifts within the congregation and to enhance the expertise of those using them.

We attempted to fulfil those aims – though in retrospect we were trying to do more than was realistic in one weekend – by way of talk and discussion, practical music workshops, preaching at one service followed by a congregational lunch at which there was an opportunity to ask questions, and then a final question panel consisting of people representing the different traditions and emphases in the church.

The questions we were asked revealed the issues and tensions that we, and many other churches, face. Here are some examples:

○ Is there a place for the choir while using modern choruses and hymns?

○ How can we grow in understanding of other traditions which are unfamiliar to us?

○ Generally speaking, people who have worshipped for a long time are happy to chant the Psalms and people who are new Christians are not. Should we therefore try to hang on to chanting, or hope to see it die a natural death?

○ How can we work towards a greater combination of musical styles in services rather than having everything in separate compartments?

I guess that every church, of whatever denomination, would reflect similar tensions and issues. In his letter setting out some observations on the weekend, Robin Sheldon wrote to me as follows:

When the Holy Spirit is allowed to move amongst a fellowship, it is difficult to control the speed of movement. For some the question of style and language is also very near the bone. This area is not an easy one, and I can see how very sensitive you need to be. I would suggest that the importance of the old language is probably too high for some, and possibly they are holding on to the culture part as a main prop. But as Christ moves graciously in people's hearts I believe He gives them new vision to focus on the real needs in worship. This is definitely a gift from above.

I was especially delighted to see how the folk in the music group and the choir began to get together over the weekend. I feel this should be encouraged further in establishing a unified approach within the music making in the church.[15]

I share those experiences in detail because it may help and give hope to others. I have to stress again that the key is to have established that Jesus is the Lord of the church and thus of the music and the worship, and that we are not trying to be partisan, personal, or get our own point of view over – that way leads only to disaster.

## Worship – here and hereafter

As we consider the fifth way in which the lordship of Jesus will affect our worship we need to be reminded that our worship here on earth is but a faint reflection of the worship in heaven. Yet our worship here and now is to prepare us for the worship in heaven above. In the book of the Revelation we have a record of that worship:

> They sang a new song:
>     'You are worthy to take the scroll
>         and to open its seals,
>     because you were slain,
>         and with your blood you purchased
>             men for God
>         from every tribe and language and
>             people and nation.
>     You have made them to be a kingdom
>         and priests to serve our God,
>         and they will reign on the earth . . .
>     'Worthy is the Lamb, who was slain, to receive power and wealth and wisdom and strength and honour and glory and praise!'
>
> (Rev 5:9–10,12)

Here is a glorious expression of worship that draws people together from every part of the world. Every eye is centred upon the Lord Jesus as the Lamb of God who has become the Lion of Judah and is seated at the right hand of power as Lord. The worship is an uninhibited celebration of who he is and what Jesus has done. He has revealed God's purposes, redeemed God's people, restored them to the position as kings and priests which the Father had planned from the beginning, and now he is reigning in glory. Unrestrained praise and adoration comes from the hearts and mouths of every single person. The whole universe praises God and the Lamb because of their work in creation and redemption; it is 'a great burst of triumph and exuberant joy in three doxologies'[16] (see Rev 4:11; 5:9–10,12–14; 7:11–12).

When Jesus is seen as the Lord of glory in heaven, then we shall begin to reflect something of his lordship in celebration and worship, in praise and in silence, in confession and adoration in our worship here below.

## Building our worship to the Lord

Let me try to sum up this chapter and theme with a picture. It is the picture of buildings. Now I suppose that buildings are another 'no-go area' for people on the subject of worship. You mustn't take the pews out, remove the chancel railings or tamper with the fabric in any way! Little do such conservationists know that liturgy and buildings have always been changing, and I imagine always will! But back to buildings – and this time the ones mentioned in the Bible in relationship to worship. In the Old Testament we have mention of the *tabernacle* (Exod 25–30), *Solomon's temple* (1 Kings 6–7; 2 Chron 3–4), Ezekiel's vision of the *new temple* (Ezek 40–43), the *rebuilding* of *the temple* under Ezra and Nehemiah, and the writings of Haggai and Zechariah, and then the building of *Herod's temple*, built between 19–9 BC to curry favour with his Jewish subjects and then destroyed in AD 70 by the occupying Roman forces. Once the new covenant between God and man is established through Christ the temple is no longer required.

A fascinating point that emerges from a detailed study of these buildings is that there is a continuity between them all. The fundamental purpose God had in calling for each building was that he might dwell in the midst of his people (e.g. Exod 25:8; 29:42–46; 40:34–35). When the tabernacle was constructed it was so that God might provide a visual aid to show that he was dwelling in the midst of his people. The tabernacle was laid up in the temple when a permanent site was established (1 Kings 8:3–9). The temple was destroyed and then rebuilt, and then later replaced by Herod's temple. Each time it was to be the focus for God dwelling in the midst of his people.

When in the New Testament the temple building was destroyed, it coincided with the coming of the new era of Christ, 'Immanuel, God with us'. God dwelt spiritually among his people. People, instead of places became the dwelling place of God (1 Cor 3:16–17; Eph 2:19–22). This earthly witness to God will be fulfilled in the heavenly temple, the New Jerusalem, when God's people will dwell eternally with him (Heb 9:24; Rev 21:3,22; 22:3). 'The dwelling of God is with men, and he will live with them. They will be his people, and God himself will be with them and be their God' (Rev 21:3).

So often it is the externals to which we cling and in which we find our security – buildings, patterns of worship, styles of music. They influence our worship rather than the God we worship influencing the externals. This is a travesty of the worship that God looks for and longs that we should enjoy – that is, worship which stems from Jesus being Lord, and which results in God by his Spirit dwelling in the midst of his people. Such worship is focused upon particular acts of worship, but will flow out into a kaleidoscope of activities which express our attitude of worship towards the Lord Jesus wherever we are and whatever we are doing. That outflow and overflow will be our concern in the rest of this book.

# For personal reflection or group study

1 In what ways do you think that your understanding of 'worship' has been altered by reading this chapter?
2 What changes do you believe need to be made in your corporate worship services or your own worship as a Christian?
3 How do you think it best to bring about these changes?

# 3 LET THE CHURCH HEAR HIS VOICE

The theme of the International Congress on World Evangelization held in Lausanne in July 1974 was 'Let the Earth hear His Voice'.[1] Some four thousand Christians from one hundred and fifty-one countries met in Switzerland with the primary purpose of continuing and completing the task of fulfilling the great commission.

Before the earth can hear, the church must hear the voice of God, and most of us are not very good at listening! I have written elsewhere about the individual Christian listening to the Lord.[2] In this chapter, I want to deal with the church as the body of Christ listening to the voice of her Lord and Master.[3]

Lord Stuart Blanch, the former Archbishop of York, has pointed out how little the disciples actually did when they were with Jesus during the three years of the Lord's earthly and public ministry.[4] They did practically nothing, but they were 'with him' (Mk 3:14). Peter, James and John were not to launch into a ceaseless round of events and activities and plans and programmes, debates, committees, reports and special events – which seem to have become the features of our churches at the end of the twentieth century. Rather they were to be with the Lord, to watch him, wait upon him and listen to him. We must recover this essential dimension in our church life today.

We need to be those who are able to hear what the Spirit is saying to the church, and for most of us that is hard. I want, therefore, to examine some basic assumptions that I am making, so that we might more easily hear the Lord speaking to his church.

## Some basic assumptions

### *God speaks today and in every generation*

One of the distinctive features of the Christian faith is that our God speaks to his people. The Christian faith delights in the scriptures as the revelation of God, once and for all given to the saints (Jude 3). This same unchanging word is the living word, and in harmony with it God will speak through his Spirit today to his church. The writer to the Hebrews tells us that 'the word of God is living and active. Sharper than any double-edged sword, it penetrates even to dividing soul and spirit, joints and marrow; it judges the thoughts and attitudes of the heart' (Heb 4:12). When reading the same Bible passage together, the members of any study group can find that God speaks to each one of them in different ways. Or in those churches where there is a regular and systematic preaching of the word of God, people testify to the way the scriptures speak to them. The preacher is sometimes embarrassingly accused of knowing all about a person and preaching accordingly from the pulpit. He has to explain that it is the word of God at work in their hearts and minds. It is a powerful demonstration that God still speaks to his people.

We also find that God speaks to his church through the different gifts of the Spirit which the church is rediscovering today. As Paul explains in 1 Corinthians 12:7–11, the gifts of wisdom, knowledge, prophecy and tongues with interpretation are all God's love gifts to his church to help us hear more clearly what he is saying to today's church.

As a local church, we passed through a period when God was speaking consistently to us about the need to give him his rightful place, to step out in faith, and to surrender our fears, after which we would move forward corporately.

We have to admit that after a period of receiving many 'words' from the Lord, we passed through a dry period of about fifteen months when God did not speak in a way that we could hear because we had not yet taken any notice of, and had not responded to, what he had already spoken to us. But then God had mercy upon us. He had been amazingly patient with us.

During our week of prayer in January 1985, it seemed abundantly clear, through a particular word of prophecy given late on the Friday evening half-night of prayer, that God had spoken and that we did not need to wait further on the Lord at that time:

> My children, you know but a small fraction of the love that I have for you, but I will reveal more of my love to you. As you reach out to one another you will know my love flowing between you. As you reach up to me, you will know my love flowing into you. As you reach out to the world you will know my love for the world which is rushing headlong to disaster. It is my world. I made it, and I do not want anyone to perish. And I need you, my people, to show my love to the world.[5]

We are learning to weigh and test what God was speaking to us. Was it in harmony with the scriptures, was it relevant to our church situation, was the person through whom God's word came open to receive his word? It was quite clear that the Lord had spoken and that this time we had not only heard but had responded – as I have recorded earlier in the book.

## God speaks because he has a will and purpose for his church

This will and purpose shall lead it in the ways of fruitful service. This, after all, is his right as the head of the church; it is also the record of the early church, and it characterised the relationship and experience of the Lord Jesus himself with his heavenly Father.

It is the right of the Lord, as head of the church, to speak to his people, and it is the responsibility of the body to seek to know the mind of the Lord. 'We will in all things grow up into him who is the Head, that is, Christ. From him the whole body, joined and held together by every supporting ligament, grows and builds itself up in love, as each part does its work' (Eph 4:15–16).

The history of the early church reveals that all effective work and advance stemmed from listening to the Lord and responding to his voice. It was when Saul, on his way to Damascus, heard the voice of God, stopped and responded, that the ardent persecutor of Christians became the utterly committed follower of Jesus (Acts 9:1–22). It was when Peter, with all his preconceived ideas and convictions, heard the Lord say, 'Get up, Peter. Kill and eat' (Acts 10:13) in response to the vision of the great sheetful of animals let down from heaven, that God broke through the racial and religious prejudice of the church, and revealed that the gospel was for the Gentiles, as well as for the Jews (Acts 11:1–18; 15:7–9). It was when the church in Antioch was waiting in worship and fasting, seeking the Lord about the next move, that 'the Holy Spirit said, "Set apart for me Barnabas and Saul for the work to which I have called them." So after they had fasted and prayed, they placed their hands on them and sent them off' (Acts 13:2–3). Thus began the first missionary journey.

The apostle Paul had learnt this basic lesson of listening to the Lord's leading. We find in Acts 16 that he wanted to know the next move in his missionary career. While we do not fully understand what was involved, we are told that he and his companions were kept by the Holy Spirit from preaching the word in the province of Asia. When they tried to enter Bithynia, 'the Spirit of Jesus would not allow them'. But during the night Paul had the vision of the man of Macedonia standing and begging, 'Come over to Macedonia and help us.' They concluded at once that God was calling them to preach the gospel to the Macedonians (Acts 16:6–10).

Here is a vital truth. We must allow the Lord to speak to his church and reveal his will if we wish to avoid frustration and achieve fruitfulness in our church life today. This is only to follow the example of the Lord Jesus himself. He set aside time to listen to the Father, and he also regarded the scriptures as the Father's word to him. He taught

that the scriptures are the authoritative will and word of
God.

Just as the scriptures bear witness to the Lord Jesus (Lk
24:27,44), so the Lord Jesus bears witness to the scriptures.
His view, simply, was that the Old Testament was his Bible;
he regarded it as the word of God. What the human writer
wrote, God said. Jesus used it as the supreme authority in
people's lives. He taught that the apostles would be given
the gift and authority and ministry of the Holy Spirit as they
wrote and spoke, so that what they would speak, God
would speak. He believed that the scriptures could not be
broken, and that they were the very power of God which,
among other things, would be God's word to him – and
to us – in temptation, suffering, behaviour and in
counselling.[6] When we truly acknowledge the lordship of
Jesus, we shall need to align our attitude to the scriptures to
his attitude.[7]

In the same way that Jesus was called upon to listen to the
voice of the Father, so the church is called upon to listen to
the Lord today. In the parable of the sower, Jesus teaches
us that it is important *how* we each listen to and receive
the word of the Lord (Lk 8:4–15). We are to listen with
attention. We are to listen with an obedient heart – ready to
respond to the word. Moreover, we are to receive the word
with single-mindedness. Luke, in his account of the parable
of the sower or soils, warns of the dangers of being like seed
that falls among the thorns. This represents those who
hear, but who, as they go on their way, 'are choked by life's
worries, riches and pleasures' and do not mature (Lk 8:14).
The last picture, that of the seed sown on the good soil, is
the picture of the Christian who gives his whole attention to
God's truth, and with patience insists and persists in following it, and so brings forth fruitfulness in his daily life. While
every Christian should seek to become like the good soil,
the Bible makes it clear that the recognised spiritual leaders
of a church – whether they be national, international or
local church leaders – have a solemn responsibility to wait
upon the Lord to hear his voice. Moses, for example, had
to wait upon the Lord to know his instructions for the

people. 'When Moses went and told the people all the Lord's words and laws, they responded with one voice, "Everything the Lord has said we will do". Moses then wrote down everything the Lord had said' (Exod 24:3; cf. 15:25–26). It seems to me that this is a marvellous example for all church congregations. So, I believe, it is the task of church leaders today to wait upon the Lord and to know his leading and purpose for his church. It is a solemn responsibility and a glorious privilege for the Christian leader.

## It is essential that the church learns to listen to the Lord

We are not permitted the freedom to do what we like and what seems right in our own eyes. It is all too easy for us to think and speak and act as if the church were *our* church, *my* church, the church that belongs to the community, and forget that the church – universal and local – belongs to Jesus. He is the head and we are the body.

It is revealed in both the Old and the New Testament that God's blessings come upon those who listen and obey his word, and his judgement upon those who fail to hear and respond. The story with which Jesus concludes the sermon on the mount – the man who built his house on the rock and the man who built it on the sand (Mt 7:24–27) – was told to illustrate precisely this point.

Therefore everyone who *hears* these words of mine and *puts them into practice* is like a wise man who built his house on the rock . . . But everyone who *hears* these words of mine and *does not put them into practice* is like a foolish man who built his house on sand.

(Mt 7:24–26)

This truth is recorded throughout the Bible, for example:

○ God called Abraham and Sarah to listen and to obey, so that through them he might bless all the peoples of the earth (Gen 12:1–3)

- ○ Renewal and restoration would come upon God's people in the Old Testament as they listened and responded to the word of the Lord (Ps 85:6–8; Ezek 37:4)
- ○ The Psalms are full of promises of the blessings that come from listening to and following the word of God. 'Your word is a lamp to my feet and a light for my path' (Ps 119:105). It is through listening to the word of the Lord that we find rest to our souls (Heb 3:7,15–18)
- ○ It is by hiding God's word in our hearts that we are able to resist sin (Ps 119:9–11). The very relevant question is asked: 'How can a young man keep his way pure?' The answer, 'By living according to your word . . . I have hidden your word in my heart that I might not sin against you'. I once heard a memorable talk on this text at a CSSM beach mission in Bude, Cornwall. The preacher[8] reminded the congregation to have the best book (the Bible) in the best place (the heart) for the best purpose (that we might not sin). Hearing the word of the Lord would lead to holiness and happiness in daily living.

The Bible contains many more promises and illustrations of God's blessing which comes when we listen to and obey the Lord. By contrast, we are also warned of the trouble and judgement that comes when we refuse to hear, and harden our hearts against God. In the Old Testament there was no prophet more burdened that God's people, priests and leaders were refusing to listen than Jeremiah (Jer 13:10,17; 19:3; 23:18–22; 25:4,8; 44:24–26). No wonder Jeremiah has been described as the 'weeping prophet', and who through his own personal experience of rejection – rejection by his family, friends, contemporaries, the leaders, the king, by society in general and the religious leaders in particular – would understand in a way that few of the prophets would what it must be like for God to feel the rejection of his word by his people. It matters to us – to our blessing and welfare – whether we listen to God or not.

There are, then, these three basic assumptions behind the need to listen to the Lord. God speaks today, because he has the right to reveal his will and purpose for his church and his world. It is the special responsibility of the leaders to discern what God is saying, and it matters intensely that we *do* listen to the Lord. Thus there follows the need to find out what are the right attitudes that the church is to adopt when listening to the Lord.

## The right attitudes

Jesus warns us, 'There is nothing hidden that will not be disclosed, and nothing concealed that will not be known or brought out into the open. Therefore consider carefully how you listen. Whoever has will be given more; whoever does not have, even what he thinks he has will be taken from him' (Lk 8:17–18). Elsewhere Jesus expounds the same dynamic spiritual principle of his kingdom: as we listen to and receive and respond to his truth in obedience, so we shall be able to receive more and more, and will grow and increase (Mt 13:12). But if we hear and listen yet refuse to respond and obey, we shall lose what we thought we had, and our ability and capacity to receive will become smaller and smaller. This is the law of spiritual development or of spiritual decline, and the key is our attitude in listening.

The New Testament makes the same point when it uses the phrases, 'He who has ears, let him hear' and 'He who has an ear, let him hear what the Spirit says to the churches' (Mt 11:15; 13:9,43; Rev 2:7,11,17,29; 3:6,13,22).

The Greek language is a rich and descriptive language, and W. E. Vine[9] describes the different Greek words which we translate 'to hear'. The usual verb, *Akouo*, means to hear a voice. It is speaking of a perceived event: we hear something. But there are six other words which we would also translate as 'to hear', each illustrating a different attitude in hearing. We listen in order to obey, or we hear so as to answer, to hear fully, to hear with favour upon, to listen with attention, to overhear or hear imperfectly. If the first speaks of the *act* of listening, the other words speak of our *attitudes* in listening.

The account of Samuel first hearing the voice of the Lord

(1 Sam 3) is very helpful and instructive for us. The background to the story is illuminating. Samuel was the son promised by God to Hannah and Elkanah, and an answer to the prayers of a barren wife. Samuel was therefore dedicated to the Lord from his birth. He grew up in the modern equivalent of a cathedral choir school – the tabernacle – where he was to receive both his spiritual and his general education under the tutorship of Eli the priest. Eli was an old and sad man. His own sons were wicked, the other priests were selfish, and the people were ungodly. It was a rare thing to hear the word of the Lord. It was in that situation, and in the quiet of the very early morning, that God chose to speak to Samuel. Samuel, so we are told, did not realise that the Lord was speaking and, like all of us, he had to learn to recognise the voice of God. 'So Eli told Samuel, "Go and lie down, and if he calls you, say, 'Speak, Lord, for your servant is listening.'"' So Samuel went and lay down in his place. The Lord came and stood there, calling as at the other times, "Samuel! Samuel!" Then Samuel said, "Speak, for your servant is listening"' (1 Sam 3:9–10). From this and other passages we discover that being ready to hear God speak requires that we wait (Job 32:11; Ps 37:7; 62:1,5; 123:2). God asks us to give him time. We have no right to expect that we can turn to prayer and demand that God speaks to us. He requires that we listen to him. Such an attitude also demands that we are silent before him with no talking. That is not easy for many of us, because we may not be familiar with the discipline of silence, and we feel we have to cover our inactivity with talk. Groups of Christians and their leaders are finding more and more that God speaks when we wait in silence before him, longing to hear his voice. Giving time in silence to listen to God involves trust and expectancy, and God will not disappoint us.

Not only can we learn from Samuel how to listen, but also how to respond once God has spoken. Samuel was terrified. God had said things that Samuel was frightened to pass on. Fortunately, Eli had taught Samuel the proper response of obedience and had warned him of the danger of hiding what God had said, so that Samuel now stepped out in faith and passed on to Eli everything God had said. No wonder we find the story ending with these words:

> The Lord was with Samuel as he grew up, and he let none of his words fall to the ground. And all Israel from Dan to Beersheba recognised that Samuel was attested as a prophet of the Lord. The Lord continued to appear at Shiloh, and there he revealed himself to Samuel through his Word.
>
> (1 Sam 3:19–21)

We have already seen that the people of Israel promised they would obey everything that the Lord gave them through Moses. Yet it was not long before they went back on their promise and were hardening their hearts through unbelief and disobedience. They were warned and reminded of this spiritual danger. 'Today, if you hear his voice, do not harden your hearts . . . That is why I was angry with that generation, and I said, "Their hearts are always going astray, and they have not known my ways." So I declared . . . "They shall never enter my rest"'' (Ps 95:7–11, quoted in Heb 3:7–11). As with Israel under the leadership of Moses, they were people with a great future ahead of them, and yet through a failure to listen they failed to achieve their potential and enter into the promised land.

The Jewish Christians to whom the epistle to the Hebrews is addressed were believers who had faced persecution. They should have become mature and outward looking, yet they had become stunted in their growth and inward looking in their attitude, once again failing to realise their potential.

It could be said of most churches that we have failed to realise our potential, that the real fulfilment is just around the corner, or that it will be next year . . . The problem at the heart of this familiar situation is the problem of the heart and a fear or unwillingness to listen to God.

# The practical activity involved in listening

If it is important that we clarify the assumptions we are making, and that we distinguish the right attitudes of heart and mind, then it is also important that we know how, in practice, to listen to the Lord.

There are four stages. Some we have already touched on. Others I need to develop in more detail.

## *Be willing to hear the Lord speak to us*

The history of God's people is a record of listening and failing to listen to the Lord. Sin and cursing entered into man's life because Adam refused to listen to God and chose to listen to Eve. Blessing was promised because Abraham, by contrast, obeyed the voice of the Lord (Gen 3:17; 12:1–5; 22:15–18). It has always been like that. The same choice faces leaders and churches and Christians today – to listen to the voice of the Lord or to listen to one of the many other voices that are abroad in the world today.

## *Be ready to wait for the Lord*

God may speak in a number of different ways to us today, just as he has chosen to speak in different ways throughout time. We have already seen that *he speaks through the prophets*, and that is the testimony of the New Testament itself: 'In the past God spoke to our forefathers through the prophets at many times and in various ways, but in these last days he has spoken to us by his Son' (Heb 1:1–2) and 'Men spoke from God as they were carried along by the Holy Spirit' (2 Pet 1:21). *He also speaks to us through the gifts of the Spirit* (1 Cor 12:8–10).

God gave John a revelation of his risen Son for the churches in the book of Revelation. It was to the self-satisfied, self-confident, but spiritually blind and deceived church at Laodicea that the Lord graciously chose to speak directly: 'I stand at the door and knock. If anyone hears my voice and opens the door, I will go in and eat with him and he with me' (Rev 3:20).

*God also speaks through dreams and visions; or by a burden that he impresses upon his people.* Whether it is through the truths of scripture, a word of prophecy, a specific verse of scripture or a picture, God will speak. Sometimes we are not sure what God is saying to us. We seem to be getting confusing and conflicting instructions, and so we come to the next stage.

## Be humble enough to weigh what God is saying

Writing to the highly excitable Corinthians, Paul instructed them to weigh calmly what they were hearing so that they could understand what God was saying. 'Two or three prophets should speak, and the others should weigh carefully what is said' (1 Cor 14:29). Earlier he had cautioned the church against hasty judgement of one another, ending his exhortation with these words: 'I have applied these things to myself and Apollos for your benefit, so that you may learn from us the meaning of the saying, "Do not go beyond what is written." Then you will not take pride in one man over against another' (1 Cor 4:6). The church leadership is called upon to judge what God is saying, and to come to a common mind.

## Be obedient to work it out

This is always the crunch issue. It is only when we are called to respond to God that we face the challenge of stepping out in faith. Each of us will have our personal Jordan to cross. When Joshua first crossed the Jordan with the priests and the people, he told them, 'You have never been this way before' (Josh 3:4). That seems to have become the stock reply of every fearful church member who does not want to face change or any new situation. But the way of blessing is to respond fully to the leading of God's Spirit.

May I share with you how this has worked out for us in one part of our church life? During a period of sabbatical leave I had observed, when in Australia, that the churches where the young people's work was flourishing were, by and large, those churches where a member of the church staff team or congregation was able to devote the major part of his time to this area of work.

Our own church council, after a time of prayer and discussion and consultation with other churches who had taken similar steps, decided that the Lord was leading us to appoint a member of staff with specific responsibility for the older youth work. While I was delighted with the idea of extra support in this area, I also envisaged that we would be occupied with much letter writing, countless interviews, frequent disappointments and a rather frustrating time before the right appointment could be made. (I need to add that quite apart from this I believed that we also needed to find someone who could lead us on in the kind of worship many were rejoicing in through the renewal movement.) We were praying about this need in the church, and all we were getting as God's leading were verses from the New Testament about 'signs and wonders'.

At first I did not understand how 'signs and wonders' had anything to do with the appointment of a youth leader. Then I remembered that only that morning I had been to St Andrew's Church, Chorleywood, for a signs and wonders conference and heard the vicar – Bishop David Pytches – say that sometimes he was asked by vicars if he was in touch with any potential curates, and that he also had curates asking about possible vicars. I decided that I would share our need with David. His reply was not encouraging. There was no one he knew, why not try elsewhere? Just as I thought!

Three weeks later, the phone rang. It was David. 'My own Youth Worker is feeling it right to move on to another parish . . . He leads the worship times here . . . Are you interested?' We were soon in touch, took time to meet and have a full interview and so the appointment was made.

God had been very gracious in bringing Geoff to us, and in blessing his ministry among us, but I do not want to give the impression that it is always like this!

We shall never get beyond the point where we shall need to hear the Lord's voice and know his leading. For example, I wrote the first draft of this chapter the day following a very important church council meeting where we seemed to have so much unfinished and unclear business before us.

These are some of the questions we faced: What did the Lord want us to do about replacing the house of one staff member which was becoming unsuitable for an expanding work? How should the actual church premises at the sister church be adapted to be more suitable? How should we respond to the challenge that a church of our size, parish and potential should have a membership of a thousand and not five hundred?[10] What changes in office accommodation, equipment and staffing do we need to minister to a growing work? How do we respond to the social needs of young people in an outer-London suburban area where the only communal meeting places are the pubs? How do we develop our music and worship to harmonise different cultures and experiences within the unity of the body of Christ and of the Holy Spirit? How do we turn the church inside out in effective evangelism, rather than being content with just a small trickle of men and women coming to a faith in Jesus? What is the right lifestyle for materially prosperous (by and large), middle-class believers in the world of today? How do we stimulate the congregation in meeting the need to double our giving in two years?

So the questions come, and we know that the answers will also come. It may not get any easier to hear the Lord's voice, but we have the firm conviction that Jesus is the Lord. It is his church and people – not ours or even mine – and he will lead us at the pace he knows we can manage, and in the ways that he shall choose. We need to be willing to wait upon him, to do his will and to go his ways. After all, we are his body, and he is the head with the right to lead. Again, he has promised that we are his sheep and he is the shepherd, and 'He calls his own sheep by name and leads them out. When he has brought out all his own, he goes on ahead of them, and his sheep follow him because they know his voice' (Jn 10:3–4).

As we stated at the beginning of this chapter, if the world without Christ is to hear the voice of God, then the church under the lordship of Christ must first hear what the Lord, by his Spirit, will say to the church. That really is a most exciting prospect.

## For personal reflection or group study

1  Consider the following Bible passages:

   o  The call of Samuel (1 Sam 3)
   o  The parable of the sower or the soils (Lk 8:4–15)
   o  Paul's change of travel plan (Acts 16:6–10)

   What do they teach you about listening to the Lord and hearing his voice?

2  'He who has ears, let him hear' and 'He who has an ear, let him hear what the Spirit says to the churches' are familiar refrains throughout the New Testament. As you or your fellowship wait upon the Lord, what do you believe he is saying to you about your own lives or about the church you belong to?

# 4  ONE MIND AND ONE HEART

It was the first time we had done it. The last verse of the opening hymn was ending:

> O, Jesus, we love You, so we gather here,
> Join our hearts in unity and take away our fear.[1]

Usually, we would have turned to the service of Evening Prayer in the *Alternative Service Book*. Instead, I invited the congregation to say Psalm 133 together:

| | |
|---|---|
| Leader: | How good and pleasant it is when brothers live together in unity! |
| People: | It is like precious oil poured on the head, running down on the beard, running down on Aaron's beard, down upon the collar of his robes. |
| Leader: | It is as if the dew of Hermon were falling on Mount Zion. |
| People: | For there the Lord bestows His blessing, even life for evermore. |

In a few simple words the psalmist had reminded us of God's longing for unity among his people and their leaders, he had spoken of the reasons why that unity is so important – it brings harmony and smooth relationships within the Christian body – and had reassured us that unity results in a vitality, freshness and reality within the fellowship: when God finds that situation he pours out his blessing – 'even life for evermore'. Where there is unity within the fellowship and among the brethren, the life and reality of God will be experienced.

Thus the unity of the leadership of any church – in heart and mind and purpose – is another essential aspect of and demonstration of the lordship of Jesus. Where Jesus is confessed as Lord, there the leaders of the church should profess and demonstrate their oneness in him.

Sadly, disunity, disagreement and division are more often the order of the day and, tragically, it is not unknown for members of the same church to avoid one another or seldom to speak to each other. That is not the pattern and purpose revealed to us in the New Testament – either for the leaders or for the members.


## The principle of unity

Many of the New Testament pictures of the church speak of unity. It is *one body* with every part working properly, having the same care, support and sympathy for one another. It is *one flock* and *one fold*. It is a building built upon the *one firm foundation* that can be laid – Jesus Christ. It is like a bride given in *marriage* to her husband, Christ.

It is not surprising, therefore, to find (for much of the time at least!) that the early church demonstrated this oneness in a remarkable way. (That there *were* arguments and disagreements the New Testament honestly acknowledges (Acts 6:1–7; 15:36–41; Gal 2:11–21; Phil 4:2–3). Time and again Luke, as he tells the story, says that they were all '*together*' or they acted '*with one accord*'. E. M. Blaiklok writes, 'The adverb translated *with one accord* . . . stresses a prerequisite of effectiveness too often forgotten in our divided Christendom.'[2]

Because this principle was valued so highly, we find that the apostles were often praying for, writing about and calling the church to establish and maintain its unity:

○ 'May the God who gives endurance and encouragement give you a spirit of unity among yourselves as you follow Christ Jesus, so that with one heart and mouth you may glorify the God and Father or our Lord Jesus Christ' (Rom 15:5–6).
○ 'I appeal to you, brothers, in the name of our Lord Jesus Christ, that all of you agree with one another so that

there may be no divisions among you and that you may
be perfectly united in mind and thought' (1 Cor 1:10).
o 'Make my joy complete by being like-minded, having
the same love, being one in spirit and purpose' (Phil 2:2).

Because Paul valued unity highly, he dealt with disunity
firmly. He was the main troubleshooter when there was
division in the church. He not only gave general teaching
about the need for unity among the members but also
identified specific problems. For example, Euodia and
Syntyche had fallen out with each other (Phil 4:2); though
we do not know what the problem was, we do know who
was involved.

Paul, however, is not without his own problems regard-
ing unity. The Bible paints him warts and all. He fell out
with Barnabas (who had cared for and encouraged him so
much in his early Christian life) over Mark's failure to stay
the course of the first missionary journey. It was Paul who
withstood Peter to the face over a vital aspect of gospel
truth. So whether it was truth that could not be compro-
mised (Gal 2) or another Christian's personality that he
could not accept (Acts 15:36–41), Paul knew what it was to
be involved in discord, as well as to appeal for harmony.

The early church believed in the principle of unity both
among members and among leaders.

## The picture of leadership in the New Testament

The principle of unity among the leadership is so vital in the
church as a visible demonstration of the lordship of Jesus
over his church that we need to take a little time understanding what the New Testament has to say about spiritual
leadership. We do not need to get involved in the pattern of
leadership – whether there was or was not a ministry of
bishops, priests and deacons, whether there was any distinctive 'ordination', how the leaders were chosen or
appointed or what was the ministry of women in the early
church. Those issues are very important, but they are not
germane to the matter in hand of the unity of the leadership

in a local church. What is exceedingly relevant is that there shall be a common mind and understanding about the demands that the New Testament made of its spiritual leaders.

There are five essential marks of New Testament church leadership:

## They must be full of the Holy Spirit

'Spiritual leadership can be exercised only by Spirit-filled men. Other qualifications for spiritual leadership are desirable. This is indispensable.'[3] The fact that the leaders of the early church were Spirit-filled men comes repeatedly in the Acts of the Apostles (Acts 2:4; 4:8; 6:3; 7:55; 9:17; 11:24; 13:9, etc.). Being men who were filled with the Spirit, they were aware of Christ's lordship and leadership. They longed to know more about Jesus and to make Jesus known in the world. They realised they would be involved in a real spiritual battle. They would be able to display the fruit of the Spirit and the various gifts of the Spirit in their manner of life and ministry of love. Reduced to its simplest terms, to be filled with the Spirit meant that through personal surrender to Jesus as Lord, their personalities were filled, mastered and controlled by the Spirit of Jesus.

## They must be men of prayer

Before Pentecost, Peter was the man of action, but afterwards he became the man of humble prayer and praise. He was the one who led, not only in the preaching and the resulting suffering but also in the prayers.

The same was true for Paul. The proud Pharisee whose main aim before he was converted was to persecute the young Christian church became the humble missionary statesman, brilliant theologian, ardent evangelist and passionate pastor. His ministry – to judge from his letters – was shot through and through with praise and prayer, petition and intercession, both for the young churches he founded and for the younger fellow workers he encouraged.

These two men were reflecting the place and power of prayer which they would have seen in the ministry of their master. As Oswald Sanders, himself a spiritual leader and man of prayer, has written: 'In nothing should the leader be ahead of his followers more than in the realm of prayer.'[4] Happy the Christian minister who can rely upon the personal and persistent prayer support, and presence at the prayer meetings, of his fellow leaders.

## They must be men of vision

In his book *Christian Leadership*, the warden of Lee Abbey, John Perry, tells the story of an American visitor startling the community morning worship by saying, 'If you can't see beyond the hamburger you will never eat steak!' It was, as John Perry comments, a memorable but unusual way of emphasising the need to enlarge our vision. John then continues, 'Every Christian leader needs to have vision . . . Vision is all about seeing beyond what has already been accomplished to what God has in mind for the future. Leadership without vision is doomed to mediocrity and even failure.'[5]

Vision is about discerning what God is doing, understanding what can happen when we are in harmony with the mind and purpose of the Spirit, and knowing the steps to take to make things happen. As someone has commented, there are three kinds of leaders and managers: risk-takers who make things happen, caretakers who watch things happen and undertakers who wonder what did happen. Leadership is about making things happen.

It was literally supernatural 'visions' that enabled Paul to fulfil the vision which God had set before him in the early church. Luke tells us of the vision Paul had of the risen Christ which resulted in Paul's own conversion (Acts 9:3–6, 10–12), of the man of Macedonia inviting the apostle to bring the gospel to Europe for the first time (Acts 16:6–10), and of the vision while he was facing severe opposition in the church at Corinth (Acts 18:9–11). It was a vision that enabled him to move forward as well as to stay put, and church leaders today need vision for those two purposes.

It was also a vision that dramatically opened up Peter's ministry in a direction he had never expected, and which at first he did not find acceptable – that the Gospel was not for the Jewish people exclusively, it was also for the Gentile (Acts 10:9–16; 11:1–18). Here was a vision that encouraged Peter to enter into a ministry and mission with people from a different culture and background.

Christian leaders are not called primarily to respond to the world's agenda, but to fulfil a vision and calling from the Lord. It will be vision that keeps the object clear when the going gets tough.

Sadly, too many local church and national leaders appear to be working with no vision or a vision so dim that they are not able to move from a ministry of maintaining the church into a ministry of reaching out to others in mission and evangelism.

## They must be men of faith

This is such an important principle of leadership, and an essential aspect of responding to the lordship of Jesus both personally and corporately, that a complete chapter is devoted to it (see chapter 9). Let me say at this point that leadership is called to act from faith.

When Jesus was faced with the need to feed the five thousand people in the wilderness (Jn 6:1ff), he knew what he would do, but he challenged the disciples – the emerging leaders – by asking what they would do (Jn 6:1–6). The response that the disciples gave illustrates the three ways in which every problem facing a church or an individual is answered. Philip replied with the *logical answer*: 'Eight months' wages would not buy enough bread for each one to have a bite!' Andrew presented the *available human resources* and concluded that they were not enough, 'Here is a boy with five small barley loaves and two fish, but how far will they go among so many?' Philip's logic concluded that they faced an impossible situation and Andrew's human supplies were pronounced inadequate, but Jesus revealed that *faith* was indispensable. He knew what he would do. It is this quality of faith which Jesus sees as essential to leadership.

## They must be able to take decisions

Along with debate and discussion spiritual leadership is also charged with making decisions. The buck has to stop somewhere. Frequently, one hears of churches, organisations and even dioceses crying out for leadership. Churches, individual Christians and organisations need to know where they are going. People long to share a common vision, aim and goal. Many Christians long that someone will give them a sense of purpose and help them to have a sense of achievement. All this demands leadership.

Leaders must be able to withstand opposition, misunderstanding and loneliness. They will face Satan's subtle attacks and periods of heart-searching, but leaders must lead, and the only safe way to lead is under the lordship of Jesus. As Peter puts it, the leader is called to be an under-shepherd charged with care for the flock but responsible to and in turn dependent upon the Chief Shepherd – the Lord Jesus himself (1 Pet 5:1–4). As Oswald Sanders has written:

> Once a spiritual leader is sure of the will of God, he will go into immediate action, regardless of consequences. He will have the courage to burn his bridges behind him. He must be willing to accept full responsibility for consequent failure or success, and not place any blame that might accrue on a subordinate.[6]

It has been necessary to consider briefly these five essential qualities of leadership – whether local, regional or national – because without them we have no hope of achieving the vital unity of leadership under the headship of Jesus. Those marks of leadership – lives filled with the Spirit, humble in prayer, motivated with vision, charged

with faith, and ready to lead – were found in the appointment by the apostles of the seven deacons who were chosen
to allow the work of the church to develop. 'Brothers,
choose seven men from among you who are known to be
full of the Spirit and wisdom. We will turn this responsibility over to them and will give our attention to prayer and
the ministry of the word' (Acts 6:3–4).

We must grapple with one other aspect of the New
Testament pattern, although it can give rise to tension and
disunity.

With the exception of the ministry of the Lord Jesus,
leadership is usually *corporate* in the New Testament. The
early church knew little of the dictatorial and dogmatic one
man – let alone one woman! – band. Today churches may
run into trouble if its leadership is not shared. One man
may not be willing to share authority with his other leaders;
a woman may feel that she has a word from God and is
unwilling to submit to others who will need to weigh the
word of prophecy.

Such attitudes betray either an inadequate understanding of corporate leadership, a real fear of failure and
insecurity or a proud and unbroken spirit. Lovingly but
firmly such attitudes need to be challenged, acknowledged,
confessed and amended.

Having said that, it is also true that leaders have to lead
and make decisions. The real art of leading is being able to
share and consult with others, and then to take decisions
and to act with the full support of colleagues.

If it is true that New Testament leadership is corporate, it
is also true that it is based upon gifts of ministry. The four
key passages in the epistles (Rom 12:4–8; 1 Cor 12:4–11;
Eph 4:11–13; 1 Pet 4:10–11) all show that ministry and
service flow from the gifts that the risen Christ has bestowed upon the members of the church, his body, through
the dynamic working of the Holy Spirit.

Sadly, in some churches there are tensions between
leaders who have been elected to office, staff who have
been appointed to their ministry, and others who have
neither a specific office, nor are officially appointed, but yet

are very clearly gifted by the Holy Spirit for some ministry. Happily, there is a solution to this problem. When Jesus is personally and constantly acknowledged as the Lord of his church, and each leader is willing to recognise this and submit to him, then they are able to recognise the ministry and gifts given to others and exercised by them and to submit to them because they have first submitted to the Lord.

Leadership and ministry in the church should not be regarded as a goal to be attained, but as a gift to be used. Appointment to any position of leadership is not a reward for long-term service or a step up the ladder towards greater or personal influence, but a recognition of a spiritual gift.

## Response and responsibility in the church

Hebrews 13 contains the simplest, and possibly the fullest, summary of the responsibility of the leaders towards the members of the church, and also the response of the church members to their leaders. We need to remind ourselves of this biblical pattern and its outworking, for this is the best way to prevent disunity in a local church.

### *The leaders' fivefold responsibility*

*Speaking the word of God* (v.7). Their message is to be of God and from God. Leaders are to be people of the saviour, the Spirit and the scriptures. Leaders are to be fed by and fashioned upon the word of God. Our debates and discussions are not to be about traditional and modern emphases, the old and the new, the evangelical and the charismatic, the Protestant and the Catholic, all of which represent the parties and the tensions that divide local congregations – rather leaders are to have their authority from the word of God. They need to know what the Lord is saying from the word of God through the Spirit of God to the church of God.

*Living consistent lifestyles* (v.7). There is great stress in the pastoral epistles – Timothy and Titus – upon the personal qualities of the life of any leader. Purity and holiness are the prime consideration. One full-time evangelist has written: 'The chief need of my people is my holiness.' This is the secret of power and effectiveness in the Lord's service. No leader can have a wrong relationship with the Lord or with another person without it very seriously weakening his effectiveness in Christian service. We cannot have division and disunity, resentment, bitterness or an unforgiving spirit and expect to experience the fullness of the Lord's blessing and power. Thus, the lordship of Christ will demand that we deal with any wrong relationships and restore the unity he calls for between brethren.

*Keeping watch over the lives of the people entrusted to them* (v.17). The ministry of leadership is a heavy and responsible one. We are called to care for the new Christian, search for the backslider, be sensitive to the Christian who is hurting and burdened. We are called to lead in the pastoring of the church, the mission into the world, and in worship that is worthy of the Lord. Who is sufficient for these things? All of us would have to reply, 'Not me!'

Yet, as we acknowledge the lordship of Jesus in our leadership, he supplies his wisdom, directs our energies, guides our work, reassures us and so ministers to the leaders directly and in fellowship with others. What would be an overwhelming responsibility alone, is light under his lordship. Did not the master himself invite his first leaders,

Come to me, all you who are weary and burdened, and I will give you rest. Take my yoke upon you and learn from me, for I am gentle and humble in heart, and you will find rest for your souls. For my yoke is easy and my burden is light.

(Mt 11:28–30)

*Giving an account of their ministry to the Lord* (v.17). It is a relief, and not a burden, when we understand what the scripture is saying. Our ultimate responsibility and accountability is to *the Lord*, not to the church or its members or anyone else. It is easy for us to act from the principle, 'What will "X" or "Y" feel, think or say if I do this or that, or don't do this or that?' Leaders can become men-pleasers, riddled with guilt, burdened by rushing from meeting to meeting. If only we could realise our ultimate responsibility is to the Lord, and not to the vicar or pastor. It really is marvellously liberating to be in a situation where all the leaders acknowledge the lordship of Jesus, and therefore do not need to explain or excuse themselves to one another. They are accountable to Jesus.

*Depending upon the Lord* (vv.7,8). Leaders are to have a faith which can be imitated by the people (v.7). The only way this can be possible is to realise that the very next verse reminds them that the Lord Jesus is the same yesterday, today and for ever. Not only are leaders responsible to him, they are called to be dependent upon him. He is the boss – not the minister or some layman who has had his way in the church for the last ten years! Ultimate responsibility is to Jesus as the head.

If, therefore, in humbly following him and responding to his call the church faces situations that seem impossible, we are not to blame or chide each other, we are to take our concerns to the Lord himself. After all, he put Philip and Andrew in the impossible situation of feeding the five thousand and he knew what he would do. Likewise, if he has allowed us to face such a problem he will also show us the way forward.

Leaders and led alike have responsibilities. Just as the lordship of Jesus holds the church leadership together in unity of heart and mind, so the congregation submitted to the lordship of Jesus will together respond to the direction the leaders are giving.

## The response of the people

Four short instructions are given to the people. They are to remember, obey and submit, greet and pray for the leaders

in the name of Jesus. Failure to do this is a denial of the
lordship of Jesus and the root cause of division and disunity
within the church.

*They are to remember the leaders* (v.7). Almost certainly
this is a word about the leaders who have died, but it is a
very appropriate word to congregations about how they
regard past leaders. It is jokingly said that most congregations idolise a new leader, believing he is the solution to all
their problems, criticise the leader who has been around for
some time (they have discovered he is human, weak and
fallible) and canonise a previous leader, forgetting all his
past failings and recalling only his achievements.

Most congregations need help in relating rightly to their
leaders – and this verse reminds us that we must neither
neglect nor exalt the leadership of a church, but rather
exercise a ministry of encouragement to our leaders. Our
spiritual adversary – Satan (about whom we shall have
more to say later) – uses the weapon of discouragement so
effectively against church leaders that the people need to be
faithful in their ministry of encouragement and support.
Most leaders have to confess that their main problem is a
lack of commitment from their congregations.

*They are called to obey their leaders and to submit to them*
(v.17). The leader's authority is delegated from above, not
derived from men. Thus leaders have a right and a responsibility to call for the obedience of those they lead. Such a
position has both its strengths and weaknesses. It is not my
primary purpose to recall the past discussions over such
issues as 'shepherding' and 'covering' which the Restoration movement in both America and Britain has raised, or
to counter the dogmatic attitudes that some priests in both
the Anglican and the Roman Catholic church display.
Rather, I want to apply this truth to the members of a
normal mainstream church who might be in danger of
'doing their own thing', and not recognising that the
people have a duty to respond because the leaders have a
responsibility to lead.

For example, if after careful prayer the leaders called a church to cancel the usual meetings for the next month in order to seek the Lord's will for the future direction of the church, would the church members (or some of them) maintain their programme, and allow those who wanted to spend their time praying and waiting on the Lord to do so? In other words, would a policy of peaceful coexistence be adopted, rather than that of wholly following the Lord? Would we follow compromise rather than Caleb?[7]

Again, if a church believed it should only raise money by way of prayerful and dedicated direct giving, would the local uniformed organisations belonging to that church and supported by the Parents' Committee insist upon holding their annual jumble sale?

Most of us do not have problems with the theory of acknowledging the lordship of Jesus and the right of the elected leaders to lead. It is only when specific situations affect us personally that our obedience both to the Lord and to his leaders is tested.

*They are called to greet their leaders* (v.24). The advantages of shared leadership are numerous – one advantage being that it should be possible for every church member to know and be known personally by some of the leaders. But the writer to the Hebrews calls us to greet them all. The lordship of Christ within the church, therefore, means that we should relate rightly to every leader, and they to us, whether we would naturally number them among our friends. It is so easy for differences of personality, background, race, culture and experience, and even tradition, to govern whether we get on with another Christian. We all too easily gravitate to those who see things the way we do, and unofficial groups and parties form within a church, unwittingly dividing the body of Christ. But if we are able to respect and warmly receive all the leaders, we are well on the way to preventing such a situation from becoming a reality.

*They are to pray for their leaders* (v.18). There are many times when Paul himself asked the local church to pray for him in his responsibilities and opportunities. It is said that when Stanley Baldwin was about to become the Prime Minister of Great Britain and his friends gathered round him to congratulate him, he replied: 'It is not your congratulations I need, it is your prayers.' I have observed the fact that when a man is appointed a bishop in the Church of England he is flooded with letters of congratulations and promises of prayer. I wonder how often the first flush of enthusiasm wanes to the occasional support in prayer? One of the greatest things we can do for leaders is to pray for them. I know how encouraged I am when people tell me or write to me, 'We have been praying for you.' It is not a sign of weakness to welcome this, but rather a sign of strength. Whoever the leaders are, they still need to be those who recognise the bankruptcy of their spirits, so that they are able to receive all that God longs to give them from the riches of his mercy and grace in leadership.

## But what about the problems?

The New Testament teaches us that leadership in the church should be corporate and united. Leadership has heavy responsibilities. Leaders may also expect certain responses from those whom they lead. Even though we get this right, there may still be some problems within the leadership of a local church. Under the lordship of Jesus how do we deal with them?

*Getting the right leaders*. Most congregations need to be taught about spiritual leadership in the church. When did the minister or pastor last teach the biblical standards about leadership in the fellowship? Have the congregation understood that choosing leaders is not a matter of competition between people, resulting in winners and losers, but of discerning the Lord's leading? When our own church knows we need new leaders, we share this with the congregation, calling first of all for prayer, and we pray that the people will recognise the person God is calling, and that the one being called will recognise the same truth!

*Understanding the past.* Leadership in a church is rather like marriage! Just as a new husband and wife bring the invisible luggage of the past and the hopes for the future with them, so do leaders in a church. They are people. They have successes and failures, past difficulties and present experiences. They will be different personalities. We need therefore to pray that God will give an increasing openness between the leaders to share. Is that one of the reasons why Jesus spent so much time with the twelve? Not only that they might be with him, but also that they might be with each other, and as very different people learn to appreciate each other and grow together to be a team that God could use in the future. As leaders are willing to spend time together, relax together, pray and worship, talk and debate together, and let down their masks and reveal their true selves, so God will give a deepening unity by his Spirit under his lordship.

*Division or differences?* The Bible rebukes us for our division, but allows us to recognise our differences. Our experience is that we can very easily come to any number of issues from different points of view – it does not matter whether it is buildings, the outreach of the church, the church's finance or our worship. People differ and God has made us that way. But as we start from the position of submission to the headship of Jesus, so his Spirit will bring us to a common mind. For that to be achieved certain guidelines are necessary. Not only must there be submission to Jesus' headship, there must also be the desire for unity and respect for each other. We must not dismiss one man's or woman's contribution or opinion. Neither must we listen the more intently to those in positions of honour in the locality (e.g. successful businessmen, lawyers, doctors or councillors) unless we know that they are also discerning spiritual people. We shall discover that God can bring us to a unanimity of mind as we seek the mind of the Spirit. It has been a great joy for me in the local church situation, as well as a member of the council of the South American Mission-ary Society – both nationally and internationally – to discover that every decision has been unanimous since we established the lordship of Jesus. We don't want grudging acquiescence; we want enthusiastic agreement. We are not in a game of winners and losers, but of discovering together the leading and will of the Lord.

It may be easy to write this, but it is not easy to achieve. It requires patience and it takes time. This was emphasised for us during one parish Houseparty Weekend. Two people had dreams that gave the same message. A family dreamt they were leaving for home after the weekend and were in such a hurry to get back that they had forgotten someone and had to come all the way back. The second dream was of a man a long way from home, longing to get home, and he wanted to go the shortest way home by rail, but in his dream he was shown that the quickest way home with everyone safely on board was, in fact, the long way round. Sometimes in our churches we have to take the long way round to get everyone home safely.

It is important to remember that among the fruits of the Spirit are patience and long suffering, and the Lord will release these qualities to us as we submit to him.

*Learning to listen together*. While leaders will talk much, they also need to learn to listen to the Lord and each other. This involves commitment and submission to each other, as well as to the Lord.

I first discovered the power of this point from St Paul's Church, Darien, New York. St Paul's is situated in the suburbs of New York State, and has grown remarkably both in members and spiritual effectiveness in the last ten years as it sought to live under the lordship of Jesus.[8] Bob Slossor has written of that congregation:

> Two factors were going to be required before they could expect unity to come – commitment and submission. If God was going to do anything among them they must be committed to the Head, and submitted to one another. Unity would not, therefore, be the method of finding the Will of the Lord, but the result.[9]

*Holding to the vision.* There can be various models of church leadership. These are sometimes polarised as the charismatic model and the bureaucratic model. The second is concerned with agendas, minutes, committees, reports, majority decisions etc., so often resulting in dull order without spiritual life. The charismatic model can be unstructured, just waiting upon the Lord, and seeking his will. I believe that the ideal is a model that combines the order and quiet methodology of the bureaucrat with the Spirit-led waiting upon the Lord of the charismatic – the structure and the Spirit, the life and the lists, the fire and the fireplace together. Whatever the model, we shall constantly need to hold firm to the lordship of Jesus. We have found that although we look back and rejoice in the events of January 1985, we need to affirm them daily and personally. As Paul puts it in his letters – we need to hold fast to the head.

We also need to hold fast to the cross, because the true place of unity is the empty cross to which we come as sinners; and the true purpose and power for unity is found in the empty tomb to which we come as disciples. Unity is found through both.

Let me close this chapter by quoting from Northern Ireland, where division and tension between north and south, Catholic and Protestant, is surely a byword to the rest of the world. Through the work of the Renewal Centre at Rostrevor, true peace, reconciliation and unity has been found. The secret is found in the cross. Cecil Kerr, the leader of the work, writing in November 1985,[10] drew attention to the reconciliation that comes through the cross.

> In our experience of the past eleven years we are convinced that the only way to peace in our troubled land and in the world is through the Cross of Christ. These words from Ephesians 2 have been a constant inspiration to us – giving us hope and courage through many difficult times.
>
> For Christ Himself is our way of peace. He has made peace between us Jews and you Gentiles by making us

all one family, breaking down the wall of contempt
that used to separate us. By his death he ended the
angry resentment between us. Then he took the two
groups who had been opposed to each other and made
them part of himself: thus he fused us together to
become one new person, and at last there was peace.
As parts of the same body, our anger against each
other has disappeared, for both of us have been recon-
ciled to God. And so the feud ended at last at the cross.

Billy and March represent so many who have been
caught up in the violence which has caused so much
suffering. One is from a Roman Catholic background,
the other from a Protestant background. Through different circumstances they came to the Cross. In serious
illnesses they each received physical healing. I saw them
stand together before thousands of people in Dublin to
witness that the greatest miracle was not their physical
healing. In their personal encounters with Christ their
hearts had been changed from bitterness to forgiveness;
from hatred to love.

Just as the cross of our Lord Jesus is the bridge over the
troubled waters of personal hopelessness and the highway
to peace in a divided world for Northern Ireland, so the
cross is also the place where leaders come together as
sinners before God, the empty tomb is the place where we
rejoice that the master is alive, and the Mount of Olives is
the place where we kneel together to receive afresh his
commission and the power of His Spirit to fulfil through his
body, the church, the mission and command of the master.
Before we go out into the world, we come together to love
one another as he has loved us.

# For personal reflection or group study

1 Meditate upon Jesus' great prayer in John 17:1–26, especially
  verses 20–26. What is Jesus' burden about the unity of his
  church, and what reasons are given for this concern?

2 In what ways in your own local church and fellowship do you
   need to put into action some of the Bible's teaching about local
   church unity set out in this chapter?

3 We must not ignore the wider dimension of church unity –
   between different churches in the local area – whether the
   churches be Catholic, House Fellowships, or breakaway groups
   from your own church. How can you extend and express the
   unity of the Spirit under the lordship of Jesus to your fellow
   Christians?

# 5  THE CHALLENGE OF MISSION

If we are not taking an active part in Christian witness, we are not just ineffective, we are positively in revolt against Christ. It is sheer hypocrisy to pay lip service to the Lordship of Jesus if we do not heed His command to evangelise.[1]

If we would apply the lordship of Jesus to every area of our church and personal lives, then we have to face the challenge of mission. That will raise three basic questions: What do we mean by mission? Why should we be concerned with mission? and, What will be the practical implications of mission for us?

## The meaning of mission

Jesus describes himself in John's gospel – on four occasions at least and in four consecutive chapters in the gospel (Jn 5–8) – as 'the sent one'. The Greek word is *apostolos* from which we get our word 'apostle'.

On the first Easter Sunday the risen Lord came and stood in the midst of his disciples and assured them of his peace.

> After he said this, he showed them his hands and side. The disciples were overjoyed when they saw the Lord. Again Jesus said, 'Peace be with you! As the Father has sent me, I am sending you.' And with that he breathed on them and said, 'Receive the Holy Spirit.' (Jn 20:20–22)

Jesus brought to his disciples his peace, his purpose and his power as they faced a new beginning in the history of the world and a new challenge in their own lives.

As the Father sent Jesus, so Jesus sends us. The ministry

of the disciples and the church is to continue the ministry and mission of the living Lord.

How do you sum up Jesus' mission? The church has often been confused and uncertain in the answer it should give. The best solution to the problem is to ask Jesus himself why he was sent. His answers were these: to bring sinners to repentance (Lk 5:32), to minister to the needs of others, to seek and to save those who are lost (Lk 19:10), to give life in all its fullness (Jn 10:10), to bring light into a darkened world (Jn 12:46), to save sinners (1 Tim 1:15), to destroy all the works of the evil one (1 Jn 3:8), and to be the saviour of the world (1 Jn 4:14). He came not to be served, but to serve, and to give his life as a ransom for many (Mt 20:28; Mk 10:45).

Jesus came proclaiming the good news of God. 'The time has come. The kingdom of God is near. Repent and believe the good news!' (Mk 1:15).

Jesus came proclaiming the good news of the kingdom of God, that is his rule over the lives of men and women throughout the world. He came to minister to the needs – physical, mental and spiritual – of every person in this world, to save the lost for the world to come. He came to teach, to heal, to save and to restore people. Perhaps the simplest way to sum up the mission of Jesus is with the phrase, 'to save and to serve'. Jesus came with the message of salvation and with the ministry of service.

Mission is not just preaching the good news of Christ in order that people will respond, neither is it simply a way to improve the conditions in which people live in the world. It is both. In his public ministry Jesus went about teaching and preaching and 'doing good and healing' (Mt 4:23; 9:35; Acts 10:38).

I believe that this biblical, balanced, spiritual and social commitment in mission is fully shown in the mission that I know best, that is the South American Missionary Society, whose work in Latin and Central America and the Iberian Peninsula of Spain and Portugal is supported by the church in Britain, Australia, the USA, Canada, New Zealand, South Africa and Ireland.[2] The Anglican church in Latin

America is concerned with establishing new church congregations, evangelistic work among students and young
people, maintaining social work among the children of the
cities, rural and agricultural work (including the establishment of basic land rights for previously deprived people),
educational work, medical work (concerned with TB hospitals and a school for the deaf), theological training and
the encouragement of national and local leadership.

## Why we should be concerned with mission

### *Because mission is the concern of God – Father, Son and Holy Spirit*

The foundation for the mission of the church rests not upon
a few key texts at the end of the four gospels (Mt 28:16–20;
Mk 16:15–18; Lk 24:46–49; Jn 20:21–23) but upon the very
character of God himself.

The Bible reveals the missionary heart, purpose and
passion of the three persons of the Trinity.

*The missionary purpose of God.* One major theme that can
be traced throughout the Old and New Testaments is the
covenant of God. The divine covenant is not like a business
deal or a marriage contract, or even the agreement to buy
and sell a house – all of which require two parties to enter
into the covenant before it can be ratified. God's covenant
is a unilateral declaration by a sovereign God of his grace
towards people.

Even in times of rebellion and rejection that is God's
unchanging attitude towards the world. As Jeremiah proclaims, God has loved his people with an everlasting love: 'I
have always loved you' (Jer 31:3 GNB). Thus the mission of
the church is to go into all the world with the message of
salvation and the ministry of service which rests upon the
unchanging missionary purpose of God the Father.

*The missionary programme of Jesus.* It must be abundantly
clear that the ministry of Jesus was one of constantly caring

for the varied needs of people. Jesus was continually 'going out' to people in Jerusalem, Galilee, Nazareth and further afield.

Oswald Sanders has posed this question concerning the unceasing missionary programme of Jesus:

> Have you ever endeavoured to calculate the extent of His travels or the magnitude of His labours during His brief ministry? In the many tours recorded in the Gospels it is estimated that He travelled on foot about two thousand five hundred miles during the three years, and we need not conclude that every journey was recorded. These were not unbroken marches, for he constantly stopped to help and heal, to teach and preach.[3]

What Jesus began to do in ministry and mission, he promised his church and disciples would continue. 'I tell you the truth, anyone who has faith in me will do what I have been doing. He will do even greater things than these, because I am going to the Father' (Jn 14:12). The challenge to continue the mission of Jesus in God's world is no less urgent now, at the end of the twentieth century. The enormous expansion in the population of the world means that there are more people, not less, who have still not heard of Jesus. About half the world's population – around 2.5 billion people – are thought to have never heard the name of Jesus. The growth of world religions means that there is more confusion about the unique means of salvation through Jesus. The easy movement of people around the world means that virtually no church, however small or remote, is exempt from the challenge of mission, not only in other parts of the world but also upon its own doorstep and neighbourhood. Jesus longs to continue his missionary programme through his church.

*The missionary power of the Holy Spirit.* The missionary power of the Holy Spirit brings home the same message. The Spirit is revealed in the gospels as coming to teach the disciples more about Jesus and, self-effacingly pointing away to Jesus, he comes to show the world its sin and rebellion and its need to be saved from future judgement. After Pentecost the Spirit came to empower the church – to send its members and leaders out, to direct and guide its work and to be the Spirit of effective mission.

The challenge of mission comes to every Christian as we worship the risen Christ and bow before him. It comes as we understand the authority and power given to Jesus, which he delegates to his church through the Holy Spirit.

Thus the very foundation for mission lies in the nature and heart of God – the Father, the Son and the Holy Spirit. Mission is the purpose of the Father, it is the purpose of the Son and it is the purpose of the Spirit, and it should be the purpose of the church – the body of Christ that acknowledges Jesus as its head and as her Lord.

Mission is not, therefore, the additional option for the super-Christian, but the normal concern of every obedient Christian because it is the concern of God.

## Because we are concerned for people

God has created us so that we might know him and have fellowship with him. He has guaranteed this through his covenant, and the only way in which people will know this is if we tell them.

How can the basic needs of people in today's world be met if there is no preaching of the gospel? Men and women wrestle with such issues as 'Do I really matter?', 'What is the purpose of Life?' and 'Is there a God?' The true answers to these cries of the human heart will not be discovered unless there is the preaching of the good news.

People are commanded to love and worship the Lord their God, but how can they unless they hear that God has first loved them?

## Because we are concerned with God's glory

It is through obedience to the great missionary challenge that glory will be brought to the Lord. We cannot be satisfied when other gods and idols and 'lords' hold sway in men's lives – whether they are the gods of pleasure, success, possessions, power, sex, sport, reputation, materialism or whatever. All such 'gods' might appear to bring freedom, but will in practice enslave. Only the Lord will bring true freedom, and for that to happen his church must engage in the great commission – for the welfare and blessing of others, as well as for the glory of the Lord.

## Because we are concerned with the welfare of the church

How can we ensure the future of the church – its people, workers and support – unless there is the preaching of the gospel? Church growth experts tell us there are four ways in which the church will grow.[4] *Biological growth* – i.e. the children of Christian parents coming to their own personal faith; *transfer growth* – Christians who have perhaps become dissatisfied with their church or move from another area altogether into a new church; *restoration growth*, where those who have fallen away have come back to the Lord and have been restored to the fellowship of the church. All these are very important, but the key to church growth is surely the fourth – *conversion growth*. This happens when new people hear the good news of the kingdom and respond to Christ and become his disciples. It is the key to effective church growth, and it is this kind of growth which is happening in parts of the world like Latin America, Africa and Asia. Nowhere is this more true than in the island state of Singapore, where in the last fifteen years since 1970 the number of Christians has increased from two percent to twelve percent of the total population of Singapore. The key has been the witness of the church members in the power of the Spirit, in fulfilment of the great commission: 'Go and make disciples of all nations . . . teaching them to obey everything I have commanded you.' The church has gone . . . is making disciples and continues to teach. Would that this were true for every church in Britain and around the world.

Maybe the church in this country has to be brought low before God and made to realise that, if it is for no other reason than its very existence, we must fulfil the great commission – otherwise the church will die.

## Because Satan will do all in his power to frustrate God's plans

Satan will try to frustrate the fulfilment of the missionary challenge and the work of God's church throughout the world. If he can dull the minds of congregations from seeing the need, from understanding the challenge and from hearing the call to respond, he will have won a victory. If Satan can get missionaries back home through illness or failure or some personal problem, he has won a victory. If Satan can tell the church that the task is too big and the responsibility too great, then he has won a victory.

We need to recall that those who have professed Jesus as Lord know their master has won the victory already. We can be victorious as we face the missionary challenge.

## The practical implications of mission

There is no calling in the whole of life that is more demanding, and yet more rewarding, than the call to be involved with mission. But what, in practical terms, should it mean for the church and all her members at the end of the twentieth century?

## Being involved in mission challenges us to reflect the unceasing compassion of God

Jesus was involved with mission because he knew and reflected the compassion of God his Father:

When he saw the crowds, he had compassion on them, because they were harassed and helpless, like sheep without a shepherd. Then he said to his disciples, 'The harvest is plentiful but the workers are few. Ask the Lord of the harvest, therefore, to send out workers into his harvest field.'

(Mt 9:36–38)

The love of Jesus in his mission was reflected both in his compassion for those in need and in the prayerful call to those disciples who would become the ones he sent out. Such love and compassion provided the motivation of men like Paul and John (2 Cor 5:14; 1 Jn 3:17–18).

'Compassion' is a very strong word in Greek – *splandnizomai* – and it means 'to be moved to the depth of one's being'. Some old translations use a phrase like 'the bowels of compassion'! Jesus was deeply moved in mind and emotion and will as he faced those in pain and sickness, sorrow and sadness, those who were lost and bewildered in life. So he went out to them in his teaching and preaching and healing ministry.

It is impossible for the Christian who truly knows the love of the Lord to walk unmoved through the prosperous areas of our cities, seeing the emptiness behind the eyes of men and women; it is impossible not to be moved with compassion. It is impossible to fly over the vast conurbations of the world today without asking who is reaching those millions of men and women with the news of Jesus. It is impossible to visit the seemingly backward and forsaken rural areas of the world (whether an isolated mission hospital or a ranching station) and meet men and women just like ourselves, yet not be moved with the love of God. Of course many Christians are not able to go, and are not called to 'go' physically overseas, but that doesn't mean they cannot effectively face the challenge of mission.

## Being involved in mission means we have the same conviction about the needs of people that Jesus had

Sadly, a subtle universalism that all will be saved in the end, no matter how they have responded to the Lord Jesus, has crept into our thinking and cut the nerve cord of the gospel message. There is also a present-day loss of confidence that the preaching of the gospel is able to change the lives of people. We need to recover this lost conviction if we want to make a powerful contribution to mission. Archbishop William Temple once said, 'If the Gospel is true for any man, anywhere, it is true for all men everywhere.'[5]

It is the testimony of one local church that the teaching and preaching of the gospel truths and a biblical statement about mission turned that church inside out. 'We saw what had been a parochially minded inward-looking congregation catch the vision of the world's need and begin to pray continually and to give generously to meet that need.'[6] Once a local church has acknowledged the lordship of Jesus it will begin to take seriously the needs of world mission. Mission will become one of the first charges upon their prayers, time and finances. They will rejoice when God calls their leading laymen – and even their minister – to be fully involved in world mission, because they know that what they are concerned with is reflecting the very heart and mind of God himself.

## Being involved in mission means we shall be faced with the unchanging call to be obedient to the work

We are told to 'go and make disciples of all nations'. Most churches face the same subtle temptations. One is to settle for *maintaining their own work* rather than being committed to mission. We work on the basis of keeping the status quo, rather than rejoicing in the state of go. 'Go' is the word that demands being identified with the needs of men and women rather than safeguarding our own interests. So many churches, to judge from their programmes and Sunday worship and preaching, are catering solely for the faithful few to continue, rather than reaching out to the uncommitted and expecting the seeker to come in.

A second temptation we face is to be concerned with *part of the mission*. Some churches are very committed to overseas mission – through prayer and giving and splendid personal support and letter writing – but they are blind to the needs that exist upon their own doorstep. Conversely, other churches will so stress the desperate needs at home in their city, housing estate or rural area that they forget about the wider world completely. While both positions and attitudes are understandable, each one is unbiblical and does disservice to the true meaning of the lordship of Christ, who was concerned with both Jerusalem and the furthest parts of the earth (Acts 1:8). Yet another version of this temptation is to understand mission as *only to the Gentiles and not to the Jews also*. The New Testament witness is that the great commission was to the Jew first and then the Gentile (Rom 1:16; 2:9–10; 15:27). It has been said that 'the light that shines farthest shines most brightly nearer home' – whether that be Belfast or Bombay, Woodford or Warsaw. Too many Christians are spiritually short-sighted where mission is concerned. Jesus instructed us to lift up our eyes and look on the fields ready for harvest.

## Being involved in mission reminds us of God's unceasing call to every believer

Most Christians act on the assumption that it is someone else's responsibility to heed the call. But the Bible tells us to whom it is given.

In Matthew 28 we have a fourfold description of the disciples:

○ They were *believers* in Jesus (v.9). They had no formal training other than having spent three years in the company of Jesus, learning much from him by example

○ They were *obedient* Christians, commanded to 'go to Galilee' (v.10) and they had responded (v.16)

○ They were disciples who had *opened their hearts in love and worship* to the saviour (vv.9,17)

○ They were *available* to him, but we are also told that some of them doubted (v.17). What a lovely human touch. Some were not sure, they were not perfect. It is this kind of ordinary Christian whom Jesus challenges about mission.

Jesus also makes very clear what he is asking us to do.

*We are called to 'look' at the world's need.* 'Do you not say, "Four months more and then the harvest"? I tell you, open your eyes and look at the fields! They are ripe for harvest' (Jn 4:35). I still recall the emotion I experienced when I was told that there were some eight million abandoned children on the city streets of Brazil each day. I had met some of them individually. The statistic is mind-blowing. Yet we need to count people simply because people count. The Lord invites us to look both the horror and the harvest fully in the face. When we truly acknowledge the lordship of Jesus, then we shall need to have much more missionary information available to our church members, to include regular missionary focus spots in our worship, so that we are constantly sharing the latest news. We must never allow the missionary task of the church's life to be submerged beneath a welter of papers, events, sales and other things to do; we must rather bring it to the top of the agenda and keep it there.

*We are 'called to pray'.* 'Pray therefore the Lord of the harvest to send out labourers into his harvest' (Mt 9:38 RSV). Information is to lead to intercession. There is no shortage of prayer letters, information folders and prayer cycles available to local churches, but there is a dearth of faithful users. If we want to honour the lordship of Jesus, we shall be as faithful in praying for the worldwide mission of the church as we are in reading our Bibles, and I believe that should be every day. Many a missionary has testified to the joy of discovering some faithful prayer warrior who has quietly testified to the fact that they have remembered 'X' or 'Y' in prayer every day since they were called.

We need a new prayer movement within the church for worldwide mission. It has happened before and can happen again. For example, before the Great Awakening in the eighteenth century, Cotton Mather organised meetings to pray for a new Pentecost to refresh and empower the lagging Puritan movement. He spent 490 days and nights interceding for a worldwide spiritual awakening. God began to answer with the creation – in 1727 – of Count Zinzendorf's community, the Moravians, which was to have spiritual and worldwide repercussions. What a contrast that heart-burden is compared to much of our intercessory prayer!

*We are 'called to give'.* That is the repeated challenge of the Macedonian church. Paul tells how they first gave themselves to the Lord, and then from the seemingly very small resources they had 'they urgently pleaded with us for the privilege of sharing in this service to the saints' (2 Cor 8:1–5). When did anyone in our church last beg to give to the work of other churches?

If we have honestly and sincerely given to the Lord's work, God has staked his reputation that we shall be better off! Has not God also said, '"Bring the whole tithe into the storehouse, that there may be food in my house. Test me in this," says the Lord Almighty, "and see if I will not throw open the floodgates of heaven and pour out so much blessing that you will not have room enough for it"' (Mal 3:10)?

Why should missionaries be short of funds? Why should missionary treasurers and committees have to worry about meeting budgets? Why should the work be held back by shortage of funds? There are only three possible answers: a) the Lord does not mean what he says, and is a liar; b) we are disobedient and we have failed to believe the Lord's promises and honour Jesus, the Lord of mission, with our finances and substance; c) we are insensitive to the Lord's directness and are giving our money to work the Lord hasn't called us to be involved with. If world evangelism is the most important work of the church, then we should put most of our money into this department. The testimony of those churches who have given away to others is that they have never been short themselves. I believe the Lord is calling us to face this challenge again.

*We are called to 'go'*. Mission seems to get harder as you go on! Some find it hard to look, others to pray, many to give, and most *to go*, but it is to action that we are called. The Christian gospel is all about coming and going. We are to keep on coming to Jesus – whether initially in faith, or because we are thirsty (Jn 7:37) or burdened (Mt 11:28) – and we are to go as he calls us. In the early church Peter, Paul and Philip were all instructed to 'go' as the Holy Spirit directed them (see also Acts 9:15; 10:20; 28:26). Jesus told his disciples that they had not chosen him, but that he had chosen them and commissioned them that they should go and bear fruit, fruit that would remain (Jn 15:16). The missionary call is a call to respond and to act. Every local church and congregation has to face that challenge if they want to honour Jesus as Lord.

For the last twenty-five years our church has had someone on the mission field in some part of the world. Recently we faced the possibility that we might have no personally home-grown missionaries in the future. Quite clearly the Lord was calling us to act and to pray specifically that he would call out a new generation of young people – and maybe older ones as well – to be involved in the mission of the church at home and overseas.

God is beginning to answer those prayers. We have seen one member of our church called to lead a major social work among children in England, and another man, made redundant from a very senior position with the closure of the Greater London Council, called to be the financial secretary of one of our eight recognised Anglican missionary societies. Two younger members of the church are ready to go overseas. Coincidences? I don't know, but when we begin to pray we should begin to see this kind of 'coincidence' happening.

God's essential nature is one of mission. Mission flows from his heart and mind and will and purpose. He is joined in that by the Son and the Spirit. The scope, sphere and arena for mission are to be as large as the world. Mission is to be to all nations and people, from now until the Lord returns. Though cultures will change and circumstances vary, the need of man will be constant.

Also unchanging is the fact that God longs that men and women become his agents in mission. This was true in the days of the early church. It has been true in the pioneering days of men like Livingstone and Carey, or Hudson Taylor and Allen Gardiner. It will also be true, however great the growth in technology and new discoveries, in the twenty-first century. We may use video and satellite as well as radio, TV and the printed word; we may equip our mission hospitals or our missionaries in the most up to date national government hospitals with ultrasound equipment – but God still requires committed men and women for this commission.

There is only one place he will find them – within the local church. They will be men and women who have bowed the knee before Jesus as the Lord of the harvest, the head of the church and the master of their own individual lives.

## For personal reflection or group study

1 Do you agree that mission means 'to save and to serve'?
2 How would you help a Christian who did not believe they needed to be involved with world mission?
3 What *new* action do you – either personally or as a church or a group – need to take in order to respond to God's call to be involved with his mission?

# 6 THE CLASH OF
# THE KINGDOMS

No one resists and disputes the lordship of Jesus more than
Satan. Jesus came proclaiming the good news of the kingdom (or rule) of God, as we have seen, but Satan came to
challenge that kingdom and to dispute the good news.
There is a clash of the kingdoms.

Jesus came with the good news of light and life, health
and wholeness. Satan came to bring darkness and death,
sickness and sorrow. There are only two kingdoms – the
kingdoms of God and of Satan, of liberty or bondage.
There is no third way, no neutral ground. We are either
enjoying the one or enduring the other.

St Paul makes this clear when he writes to the Colossians:
'[Christ] has rescued us from the dominion of darkness and
brought us into the kingdom of the Son he loves, in whom
we have redemption, the forgiveness of sins' (Col 1:13–14).
Again, the Lord had called Paul to preach the gospel so
that people's eyes might be open and they may turn
'from darkness to light, and from the power of Satan to
God, that they may receive forgiveness of sins and a
place among those who are sanctified by faith in [Jesus]'
(Acts 26:18).

Satan would love to be regarded as the non-existent
enemy, but Jesus, more than anyone else, taught that Satan
is real; he took the full force of the devil's attacks and
opposition, won the victory over him, and taught Christians
how to respond to their spiritual enemy.

If individually and corporately we want to fully honour
Jesus as the Lord, then we need to understand three very
important issues: the reality of our spiritual adversary; the
challenge to our spiritual attitudes; the need for practical
action.

## The reality of our spiritual adversary

While the devil's origins are not completely clear (Gen 3:1, 14–15; Isa 14:12–14; 2 Pet 2:4), we do know that he is not just a vague evil force but a spiritual personality able to deceive (Gen 3:1; 2 Cor 11:3), to lie to people (Jn 8:44), to blind them to the gospel (2 Cor 4:4), to work in people's lives (Eph 2:2), to falsely accuse believers (Rev 12:10), to confuse them by appearing as an angel of light (2 Cor 11:14), or to destroy them through his work as a roaring lion (1 Pet 5:8).[1]

### *In the ministry of Jesus*

In his own ministry, Jesus encountered Satan in various ways. He met him in times of temptation after periods of great spiritual blessing (Mt 4:1; Lk 4:1). He saw the effects of Satan's work in other people's lives as he encountered the woman who had been crippled by a spirit and was unable to straighten up. Jesus described her as a daughter of Abraham, whom Satan had kept bound for eighteen years (Lk 13:16). He ministered to both the father and the son who was possessed by a spirit that robbed him of his speech and that threw him to the ground, causing him to foam at the mouth, gnash his teeth and become rigid in his body (Mk 9:17–29).

Jesus witnessed Satan's activity in the lives of his closest friends. Following his remarkable testimony that the Lord was the Christ, the Son of the Living God, Peter at once began to rebuke Jesus, contradicting him, when he taught that he must go to Jerusalem, suffer, be killed and then on the third day be raised to life. Matthew tells us that Peter took Jesus aside and began to rebuke him, 'Never, Lord! This shall never happen to you.' Jesus turned and said to Peter, 'Get behind me, Satan! You are a stumbling-block to me; you do not have in mind the things of God, but the things of men' (Mt 16:22–23). Satan used Judas in his attacks upon Jesus. At what should have been the most sacred time – the Passover meal – the devil had already prompted Judas Iscariot, the son of Simon, to betray Jesus (Jn 13:2). And then later on, as soon as Judas took the bread, Satan entered into him (Jn 13:27). John ends the account by saying that as soon as he had taken the bread Judas went out, 'And it was night' (Jn 13:30). What a poignant picture of the darkness that Satan brings to the world, and to the soul and mind of any disciple who opens his life to the devil's influence and power.

## In the history of the world

In the garden of Eden, the serpent questions the word of God: 'Did God really say, "You must not eat from any tree in the garden"?' (Gen 3:1). He questions the command, and denies the results that will follow if God's word is broken. 'You will not surely die. For God knows that when you eat of it your eyes will be opened, and you will be like God, knowing good and evil' (Gen 3:4–5). In other words, rather than punishment following your disobedience, God will bless you and you will be rewarded. From that moment onwards there is hostility between God and Satan, between the Son of God and the prince of this world; as God said to the devil: 'I will put enmity between you and the woman, and between your offspring and hers; he will crush your head and you will strike his heel' (Gen 3:15).

The book of Revelation records the spiritual battle that took place in the heavenlies between Michael and his angels and Satan and his angels:

And there was war in heaven. Michael and his angels fought against the dragon, and the dragon and his angels fought back. But he was not strong enough, and they lost their place in heaven. The great dragon was hurled down – that ancient serpent called the devil, or Satan, who leads the whole world astray. He was hurled to the earth, and his angels with him.

Then I heard a loud voice in heaven say:

'Now have come the salvation and the power and the kingdom of our God, and the authority of His Christ.

For the accuser of our brothers, who accuses them before our God day and night, has been hurled down. They overcame him by the blood of the Lamb, and by the word of their testimony; they did not love their lives so much as to shrink from death.'

(Rev 12:7–11)

A few chapters later we are told that the war will continue: 'They will make war against the Lamb, but the Lamb will overcome them because He is Lord of lords and King of kings – and with him will be his called, chosen and faithful followers' (Rev 17:14).

## Satan is a defeated enemy

The New Testament boldly declares Satan a defeated enemy. Paul writes to the church at Colosse:

[God] forgave us all our sins, having cancelled the written code, with its regulations, that was against us and that stood opposed to us; he took it away, nailing it to the cross. And having disarmed the powers and authorities, he made a public spectacle of them, triumphing over them by the cross.

(Col 2:13–15)

John affirms the same truth when he writes: 'The reason the Son of God appeared was to destroy the devil's work' (1 Jn 3:8).

The war may continue, but the victory has been won. A helpful illustration of this can be drawn from the Second World War.[2] On 6 June 1944 the allied forces invaded France and the continent of Europe, and from then on began to push towards Germany, with victory proclaimed on 7 May 1945. There were still months of very fierce battle, and many lives were to be lost, but few doubted that the landing on that June night in 1944 was the crucial victory. Likewise, when Jesus died on the cross of Calvary and rose again on the third day, the crucial battle had been fought and the vital victory had been won. Satan still pursues the fight, but Christ is the victor. Praise God that in many parts of the world the Christian church is lifting up high the banner of the Lord Jesus and letting it fly for all to see. This is the way of victory. It is lifted high in the name of Jesus, and that name holds the secret of power and success.

## In the life of the early church

Peter experienced this when confronted by the beggar asking for silver and gold at the temple gate (Acts 3:1–9). Peter protested that he had no money, but commanded him in the name of Jesus to rise and walk. To the astonishment of the crowd, and the delight and joy of the beggar, Jesus healed him, and he walked!

Paul, on the other hand, was pestered daily by a slave girl who had a spirit by which she predicted the future and brought her owners a great deal of money by her fortune-telling. Able to put up with this no longer, Paul finally turned round on her and commanded the spirit, 'In the name of Jesus Christ I command you to come out of her!' Luke records, 'At that moment the spirit left her' (Acts 16:16–18).

The Christian church since the time of Jesus has been entrusted with his power and authority to come against evil, sin, disease and all the works of Satan, and to be a victorious church.

In brief, we have sketched the Bible's teaching about the reality of Satan, the methods he uses against Christ and the believer, the certainty of Jesus' victory against the devil, and the promise of his power for every Christian. I want to devote the rest of this chapter to working out what the lordship of Jesus means in practice as we face our spiritual enemy. How should the reality of our spiritual enemy affect our attitudes, and stimulate our action?

# The challenge to our spiritual attitudes

When a man or a woman becomes a committed Christian they find their attitudes towards many areas of life being challenged. Nowhere is this more true than in the area of our attitudes to evil and sin, to temptations and to the world in which we live.

## *Towards the world in which we live*

In seeking to follow the example of Jesus in the battle against Satan, we acknowledge his lordship by having the same attitude towards the world as Jesus did. The 'world' is not people or places, but values, standards and attitudes which do not acknowledge God or confess that Jesus is Lord. Those attitudes are summarised in the beatitudes of the sermon on the mount in Matthew 5:3–10 – the inward, spiritual attitudes we are to have towards ourselves and to others if we would follow Jesus and defeat Satan.

It is the attitudes of being 'poor in spirit,' of 'mourning over sin', of 'meekness', of being 'a peacemaker', 'of seeking to be hungry and thirsty after righteousness' that Jesus looks for.

Do not misunderstand what Jesus is saying. Often the church has been marked out by inefficiency, bad publicity, shoddy organisation, inadequate administration, second-rate buildings, indifferent accommodation, dim lighting and many other unattractive features. None of these commend the saviour as Lord, and they are not commanded as part of the Christian life. But we must not put our trust in their opposites. It is the way of the world to exalt clever and slick ways, ingenious approaches, first-rate organisational ability, eye-catching publicity, charming personalities. There is nothing intrinsically wrong with them, but they are not the weapons with which we are called to fight Satan. The church that believes it can pull in the crowds by throwing out its pews and bringing in comfortable chairs, carpeting the floor and brightening up the lighting will be deceived. The world wants to know whether the good news results in better people, not better places.

It was to the 'poor in spirit' that Jesus promised the kingdom of God. The Greeks had two words for poverty. One meant that a person just had enough to make ends meet, but there was nothing left over. The other word meant abject poverty, when a person had absolutely nothing, they were bankrupt and there was no room for pride or self or boasting. It is that kind of poverty of the human spirit that Jesus is commending to his disciples. It is when we are able to say that we are nothing, that we have nothing, that we have gained nothing, and can do nothing, that we are in a position for Jesus to fill us and use us and make us what he wants under his lordship.

Every Sunday evening those taking any official part gather at 5.45 p.m. to pray for our evening service. The fact that God honoured and blessed us the previous week is no guarantee that he will do the same this week. Every time we – and I especially – have to 'come back to square one', to confess our need, to honour his lordship, to open our hearts before him. I can only testify that every time we have come spiritually bankrupt before him, he has graciously enriched us. But how hard it is for mature Christians, and especially ministers and clergy, to admit before others that they have a need. Yet the lower we come before him, the higher he will lift us up in his service. 'He who humbles himself will be exalted' (Lk 14:11; 18:14).

## Towards the influence and power of the occult

Jesus calls us to have the same attitude today as he had towards the occult and the supernatural. In Britain, the parliamentary laws against witchcraft were repealed in 1951, and occultists and Satanists have been able to pursue their beliefs and, though not officially, their practices. It is estimated that there were something like 200,000 Satanists in this country in 1986. The Australian author Christopher Koch, in his book *The Year of Living Dangerously*[3] believes that we are living in the greatest age of witchcraft and superstition since the fourteenth century. There has been a dramatic increase in the publication and use of horoscopes, and they can be found in most syndicated papers and journals. Playing with Ouija boards, consulting mediums, using tarot cards and being fascinated by spiritualists are all part of the present-day scene.

Christ's attitude demonstrates that we must neither be involved in such practices nor tolerate them: instead, we must oppose them, resist them, and act against them.

In the book of Deuteronomy we read:

When you enter the land the Lord your God is giving you, do not learn to imitate the detestable ways of the nations there. Let no-one be found among you who sacrifices his son or daughter in the fire, who practises divination or sorcery, interprets omens, engages in witchcraft, or casts spells, or who is a medium or spiritist or who consults the dead. Anyone who does these things is detestable to the Lord, and because of these detestable practices the Lord your God will drive out those nations before you. You must be blameless before the Lord your God.

(Deut 18:9–13)

In a similar way, Paul lists the works of the flesh which the Christian is not to practise: 'sexual immorality, impurity and debauchery; *idolatry and witchcraft*; hatred, discord, jealousy, fits of rage, selfish ambition, dissensions, factions and envy; drunkenness, orgies, and the like' (Gal 5:19–21).

Many in the church are realising that they must also include Freemasonry under the same heading. They believe the Christian ought to separate himself from this movement, because at the heart of Masonry is a denial of the uniqueness and deity of the Lord Jesus. Our saviour and Lord is put alongside other gods and other faiths, consequently denying Jesus' teaching that he is the way, the truth and the life, and that no one comes to the Father but by him (Jn 14:6).

There are an increasing number of testimonies from Christians about their need to be set free from their commitment to Freemasonry. Let me share just one that has its background in Africa, but would be typical of many. I am grateful to the Rev. Guy Catchpole for permission to quote his experiences.

I was a very senior member of this Satanic order in Kenya – a past master of three badges, a past principal of the Royal Arch Chapter, a member of the Rose Croex (33°), and a member of the District Grand Lodge of East Africa (the governing body for East African Masonry) – and I was ambitious for higher things in Masonry. For a long time, even after my conversion, I defended Masonry, and maintained that I was able to reconcile its philosophy and precepts – supposedly based on teaching morality and charity – with Christianity.

But in his time, and in his own gentle way, the Holy Spirit began to show me how blind I had been, and how effectively the enemy can use his weapons of subtlety and rationality in the blinding process. It was to the point of having my eyes fully open, and my heart sufficiently convicted of the evils attaching to Masonry and the powerful bondage it imposes. It was one of the hardest things I have ever had to do – getting rid of my regalia, Masonic literature and all the outward trappings of this evil craft. But this was not enough – the Holy Spirit showed that another step had to be taken in order to completely release me from the bondage I was in, and that was to approach a brother in Christ who would pray for my release. This he did, with the laying on of hands. What a beautiful sense of lightness and freedom I experienced when that oppression was lifted![4]

This is in harmony with my own pastoral experience. A growing number of Christians are discovering that they cannot fully honour Jesus as Lord of every part of their life while they continue to be involved with masonic practices, or even retain the regalia and trappings of any masonic association within their homes. They need to rid themselves of these, as do believers who once were involved with other aspects of the occult.

It is also true – apart from the specifically occult – that we cannot really know Jesus as Lord while our homes have stored away in them any compromising literature, any signs and symbols connected with sexual deviation, any pornographic material, any letters we keep that express hurts and resentments from others. Rather like the Jews in Acts 19, many churches or Christians will need to have some bonfires and burn that which dishonours the Lord. Like the Israelites of old, we shall need to grind into powder and ashes anything we have worshipped and submitted to other than Jesus.

I am not writing from theory. The Lord has had to show me that I need to destroy every hurtful letter that I might receive as a minister. So long as I filed a letter away in my study, I also filed away the comment and hurt and reaction in my heart against that person. You cannot keep such letters and experience true forgiveness at the same time. Do some church offices and clergy studies need to be cleansed if Jesus is truly to be Lord?

## Towards the problem of sickness

If we want to truly own Jesus as Lord, we need to have the same attitude that he had towards sickness and every attack that Satan brings against people. The subject of healing is a complex and controversial one in the Christian church. The ministry of men like John Wimber of Vineyard Ministries – whose teaching on power evangelism and the ministry of 'signs and wonders' has led Christians either to be enthusiastically for, cautiously uncertain, or strongly opposed to his teaching – is a case in point.[5] What is not in dispute is that during his lifetime Jesus bore witness, by action and teaching, that Satan is the origin of darkness and disobedience, he is the author of disease, he is the cause of evil spirits and demonisation, and he is intent upon the destruction of all who put themselves in his power. He intends to

bind many with the fear of death and ultimately he wants to
bring all to death.

It is equally true that in Jesus' ministry and throughout
the New Testament the Christian is commanded to resist
Satan, to rebuke him and command him to cease his works,
to drive him out from those places and people which have
given him room and to release those who are bound and
restore that which Satan has withered. We are in the
business of fighting against and reversing the works of
Satan.

## Towards the Christian church itself

Just as the saviour refused to adopt the attitudes of his day,
and thereby resisted Satan, so Christians can by their
attitudes win or lose the spiritual battle.

Consider some of the words that may well be used to
describe Christians today. They may be unbelieving, unforgiving, unwilling to allow God his way, disobedient, mean
and ungenerous, unkind and unloving, critical and divisive,
unclean and impure. Satan is very happy to have such
people worshipping in our churches, because we help him
in his work.

Clive Calver, the general secretary of the Evangelical
Alliance, has written: 'There are a number of demonic
forces at work in the church today for which we are
responsible, and which are being allowed to destroy the
holy bride of Christ.'[6] He then goes on to write about
pessimism, complaint, discouragement, negativism, intro-
version, traditionalism, etc. Commenting upon this in the
foreword to the same book, David Pawson writes: 'As I
read the manuscript I noticed that most of the symptoms
of our sickness ended with ". . . ism". Criticism, cynicism,
defeatism, pessimism, traditionalism, formalism, in-
stitutionalism, survivalism, isolationalism, negativism – the
list seemed endless. On the other hand, the positive
alternatives invariably ended with "ity". Vitality, maturity,
community, fidelity, sensitivity, humility, charity, variety,
unity – the words had a different ring about them. The best

example was the underlying contrast between the despair, which ultimately results from humanism, and the hope that is rooted and grounded in Trinity.'[7] There is the need above all to get back into the battle and to fight the enemy together instead of fighting each other separately. That is what Jesus demands and calls each of us to when we surrender to him as Lord.

## Towards temptation

We do not have to fall into temptation! Peter reminds the early Christians to abstain from sinful desires which war against the soul (1 Pet 2:11). We have the choice as to whether we abstain or indulge. Just as a man can abstain from alcohol, smoking, and many other weaknesses of the flesh, so we are able to abstain from giving way to the temptations of the devil. We need to have the same attitude that Jesus had towards the temptations of Satan, which is spelt out so clearly in the wilderness testings (Mt 4:1–11; Lk 4:1–13).

Satan came to Jesus after a time of great spiritual blessing. Jesus was alone in the wilderness of Judea for forty days with no one to share fellowship or encourage him spiritually.

The Lord was tempted to doubt his relationship with his Father and to meet his legitimate physical desire for food in the wrong way. In his first attack, Satan challenged him: 'If you are the Son of God, tell this stone to become bread' (Lk 4:3).

Satan then brought before Jesus, in a vision, all the kingdoms of the world which the devil claims he has the authority to rule. If Jesus would submit to the devil he would allow him to set up a kingdom far greater than the Roman rule, and he would avoid the cross; Jesus would be able to bring blessing to people. But the kingdoms of the world are not Satan's to give.

Satan's third attack upon Jesus was to entice him to throw himself off a pinnacle of Solomon's temple in Jerusalem, claiming the protecting power of God, and compelling faith from the people. By yielding to such a temptation Jesus would deny the very gospel and purpose for which he had come.

Similarly, Christians can be tempted to satisfy in the wrong ways the natural and God-given desires for food, sex and fulfilment. The church can so easily compromise its message and its methods to make the gospel more attractive.

Our attitude towards Satan's attacks is to be the same as our Lord's. First, he was single-minded in seeking to fulfil only the will of his Father and do those things that would please him (Jn 8:29). The place where temptation is resisted and Satan is defeated is in the mind.

It was said of Field Marshal Lord Montgomery as he fought against Field Marshal Rommel in the North African campaign of the Second World War, that he refused to consider the possibility of defeat. Monty had in his caravan headquarters a photograph of his enemy, so that he might know him and keep him in mind, but he also had in mind his enemy's defeat.

The key to victory lies in the mind of the believer. We are to have the mind of Jesus, who refused to succumb to Satan's attractive blandishments.

Second, Jesus constantly submitted his ways to the written word of God. Three times in both accounts we have the words, 'It is written . . .' Jesus is referring to the book of Deuteronomy, and quotes from chapters 6:13 to 8:3. Was he meditating upon that passage of scripture? Was he feeding his mind and soul with the food of God's word although he could not feed his body? Jesus was determined not only to conform to the word of God but also to contemplate the word of God day by day. In our struggle against Satan, if we would truly know Jesus as Lord, we must have the same knowledge and use of the scriptures.

Sadly today we have become an experience-centred generation, unwilling to submit to the regular daily reading of the Bible and then wondering why we are defeated by Satan. We are to take the sword of the Spirit, which is the Word of God (Eph 6:17), as we wrestle against our enemy.

We live in days when many new Christians come to the faith with no Christian background and no Bible knowledge. The Lord Jesus invites us to read and feed upon his word for our spiritual nourishment and strength, and churches must give more attention to the teaching of those young in the faith, to help them become strong in the fight.

There will then follow, thirdly, the blessing of knowing more of the power of the Holy Spirit. As Jesus began this period of testing, 'full of the Spirit', so, when it was over, he 'returned to Galilee in the power of the Spirit' (Lk 4:14). Luke suggests to us, in those words, that Jesus was more aware of the spiritual resources God had given him for his ministry. Shortly, Jesus was to stand in the synagogues and state that the Spirit of the Lord was upon him to fulfil the ministry given to him as the Christ (Lk 4:16–21). Resisting temptation will lead to a greater release of the Spirit's power.

Just as Jesus' attitude of resisting temptation led to his effective action in his fight against Satan, so as we have the right attitudes – which we have sought to outline – we shall find ourselves adopting the appropriate action in daily Christian living.

## The need for practical action

### *The clash of the kingdoms!*

Once we have made Jesus Lord, we shall find we are in the front line of the spiritual battle against Satan and, therefore, we shall need to wage spiritual warfare. We cannot hope to honour Jesus as Lord and at the same time avoid the spiritual battle. Paul wrote to the Ephesian Christians, demonstrating that Jesus is the Lord and the head of the church and that every believer is to be strong in the Lord and to engage in the battle (Eph 1:22–23).

Weymouth translates Ephesians 6:12 like this: 'For ours is not a conflict with mere flesh and blood, but with the despotisms, the empires, the forces that control and govern this dark world – the spiritual hosts of evil arrayed against us in the heavenly warfare.'

It should, therefore, be standard practice for every Christian to put on the whole armour of God. Some of this equipment is basic, and we are to wear it all the time. We are to have the truth of God's word around our waist – which implies a clear and basic understanding of God's word within our lives. We are to have on the breastplate of righteousness, by walking in active obedience to God's word, and we are to stand firm and ready with the sandals of peace.

When the battle is engaged we must take the shield of faith – that is utter trust in the power of the blood of the Lord Jesus to cleanse us so that no dart from Satan can penetrate our united defences. We shall put on the helmet of salvation so that our minds are protected from the lies and subtle attacks of the enemy. We shall have in our hands the sword of the Spirit – allowing God to bring us just the word he knows we need in that hour of battle, and we shall be praying in the Spirit, and rejoicing in the power and authority we have through the name of Jesus against the enemy. I fear that many Christians today know little about this battle and the practical use of the armour, and thus rarely enter into victory. If we would honour Jesus as Lord, then we must show clearly that we are on his side in the continuing spiritual battle.

## We challenge the values of the world

Once Jesus is Lord of our lives, we shall find ourselves opposed by the world systems and philosophies that exalt themselves against him.

Paul has written about the spiritual forces that influence this dark world, Jesus warned against the spirit of the world. John wrote about the standards and values of the world: those who acknowledge the lordship of Jesus will have standards and values which differ greatly from those of the world. For example, those who work in the banks, insurance houses, foreign exchanges and the money markets testify that money creates its own philosophies and standards in this world. It is also true that the local church can have the same attitude as the world does towards possessions and money.

The early church found its spiritual power increased as its members released their possessions and gave their money to the Lord's work. It was Barnabas who brought the money from the sale of a field, it was the believers of the early church who shared everything they had. They brought their possessions and put them at the feet of the apostles so that there was not a needy person among them. In the middle of these verses is the claim that the apostles continued to testify to the resurrection of the Lord Jesus with great power (Acts 4:32–35).

By contrast there is the greed of Ananias and Sapphira that led to their judgement and dishonour. The Christians of the western world today need to rediscover the blessing of a generous spirit that releases both possessions and power and enables the church to fulfil its commission under the headship of Jesus.

Christian parents who have diligently taught their children will find very different attitudes, standards and values operating within the schools and among children in the same form. Achievements, lavish far-away holidays, possessions, the things of this world, dishonesty, drug abuse and sexual licence will be commonplace. The spiritual battle is real for Christian parents and Christian children alike.

## We trust and obey the Lord

Speaking to Christian pastors in Singapore about the way of victory against Satan, Derek Prince gave this practical instruction:

Make and keep Jesus as Lord, keep the helmet of salvation guarding your minds. Live by the word of God, and do not rely upon feelings and emotions. Go on submitting to God, for that is the only way to resist the

counter-attacks of Satan. Make sure that you are in the
right fellowship that honours Jesus as Lord.[8]

That is very practical and thoroughly biblical teaching. It
follows the example of Jesus himself. The secret of Jesus'
victory over Satan was his obedience to the Father. For the
early church, victory and effective Christian living were
rooted in obedience to the Father.

For example, when Peter and John were summoned
before the Sanhedrin to explain the healing of the cripple
and why they would not obey the council's orders to stop
preaching and teaching in the name of Jesus, they
answered: 'Judge for yourselves whether it is right in
God's sight to obey you rather than God. For we cannot
help speaking about what we have seen and heard' (Acts
4:19–20).

Peter had realised, because they heard nothing other
than the Lord, that they had no choice but to obey. Jesus
taught us that if we want to rest in his love we must obey his
commands, and that if we did obey his commands we would
abide in his love (Jn 14:15; 15:10).

Linked closely with obedience is trust. Christians are not
called to blind faith; we are called to trust and obey, with
our eyes looking steadfastly at the cross, which was the
place where Jesus defeated Satan once and for all.

In the book of Revelation, the believers of the tiny
Christian church were able to survive the terrible persecution of the Roman Empire because they overcame 'by the
blood of the Lamb and by the word of their testimony' and
'they did not love their lives so much as to shrink from
death' (Rev 12:11).

Jesus has already done his part: he died upon the cross
and shed his blood. We are now called to bear witness to
what Jesus has done and to speak it out in testimony by
which we have the victory. Speaking out for Jesus means
that we are trusting him. We are burning our boats and
putting all our confidence in the Lord. He will not fail us.

Let me share two examples with you. In many parts of
the world – except in the western world and Europe at the

present time – the church is growing very significantly. It is not coincidental that where the church is spreading, its members have learnt to trust and obey and to give simple witness to the power and the love of Jesus, and to withstand the subtle attacks and temptations of the devil.

Again, one of the fastest-growing Christian organisations around the world today is the Full Gospel Business Men's Fellowship.[9] It doesn't matter where you may meet – be it London or Caracas, Venezuela – you will find that the staple spiritual diet of their meetings and the cause of their growth is the personal testimony to the Lord Jesus given by members.

Satan is powerful – we must not underestimate his power and subtlety – but Jesus' power is greater. There may be times when the spiritual forces ranged against us in our homes, work-places, schools, colleges, and even the situations we face as a church, seem to be overwhelming. But we can triumph in the Lord Jesus, who has been given a name – and an authority – above every name, because 'at the name of Jesus every knee [shall] bow, in heaven and on earth and under the earth, and every tongue confess that Jesus Christ is Lord' (Phil 2:9–11). There is going to come a time when even Satan has to confess that Jesus Christ is Lord!

## For personal reflection or group study

1 In what practical ways is the spiritual battle relevant to you in your daily life, and in the life of your church and fellowship?
2 What does it mean to you to put on the whole armour of God and to stand against Satan? (See Eph 6:11–18.)
3 How would you help the Christian who is scared by the whole idea of the spiritual battle against Satan and evil in today's world?

# 7 SERVING THE LORD

May I attempt to summarise what we have said so far in this book? Jesus Christ is the Lord and head of his church. We are called to worship him – and that will include listening to what the head has to say to the body; we are called to wage warfare against Satan; and we are called to be united together to work for our Lord and master in the mission to which we have been called. All of this is summed up briefly for us in Ephesians 4:16: 'From [Christ] the whole body, joined and held together by every supporting ligament, grows and builds itself up in love, as each part does its work.'

If that is the ideal, the reality is often very different. A black preacher illustrated this problem when he spoke in his church one Sunday on the subject of 'Bones'. He likened church members to 'Bones'. There were the wish-bones – always wishing and intending to do things, but never actually doing anything. There were the funny-bones who were touchy and easily hurt. There were the jaw-bones – the gossips and the critics in the church: lots of words and little work. There were the dry bones who were prim and proper but as dead as a door knob. There were the tail-bones who were always behind in their work and their giving, but fortunately, there were also the back-bones – who were the spiritual support of the whole church.

The Old Testament also speaks of dry bones, in Ezekiel's vision of the valley:

> The hand of the Lord was upon me, and he brought me out by the Spirit of the Lord and set me in the middle of a valley; it was full of bones. He led me to and fro among them, and I saw a great many bones on the floor of the valley, bones that were very dry. He asked me: 'Son of man, can these bones live?'

I said, 'O Sovereign Lord, you alone know.'

(Ezek 37:1–3)

Those bones were the house of Israel – the very people whom God had called out to be his servants for the work of mission and the kingdom. They were dead. But through the preaching of the word and the prayer for the reviving work of the Holy Spirit, those dry bones were transformed into a mighty army – 'So I prophesied as he commanded me, and breath entered them; they came to life and stood up on their feet – a vast army' (Ezek 37:10).

What a picture and what a promise for the church today in the service of the Lord. But how do you transform the dry bones that are often found within churches into an army for the Lord?

There are seven steps we need to take. We must:

○ Understand the purpose of the church
○ Value the membership of the church
○ Understand about ministry and gifts
○ Find our place in the church
○ Begin to use every-member ministry
○ Mobilise and train the members
○ Emphasise the importance of love

## We must understand the purpose of the church

Lent 1986 was the time of a great campaign for many of the churches in England to ask and answer the question, 'What on earth is the church for?'[1] The description most frequently used for the church is that of the body (Rom 12:4–8; 1 Cor 12:12–31; Eph 1:22–23; Col 1:24): 'Now you are the body of Christ, and each one of you is a part of it' (1 Cor 12:27). We use the word 'ecclesiastical', not to remind us that the church is a vast organisation, with its synods, councils, boards and many meetings and officials in every denomination, but because of the word in the Greek – *ekklesia* – whose primary meaning is 'the called out' ones. The church, therefore, is the body of Christ, called out

from the world and called together under the headship of
Jesus.

The apostle Paul makes it clear that the church as the
body of Christ has a threefold function. First, it is to *become
mature* and grow up. In Ephesians 4 Paul mentions the
various stages of growth through which the members of the
church go – and consequently the church itself passes.
There is infancy (v.14), then the volatile teenage or 'growing up' period (v.15) and finally maturity (v.13). Just as the
human family knows the joys and frustrations of each of
these stages, so does the church. It is to grow up. Paul
longed to present the church mature in Christ (Col 1:28).

For this to become true there has to be, secondly, *the
ministry of the body towards itself*. Christ has equipped the
body for dynamic and supernatural – yet normal – growth.
'[Christ] gave some to be apostles, some to be prophets,
some to be evangelists, and some to be pastors and
teachers, to prepare God's people for works of service, so
that the body of Christ may be built up until we all reach
unity in the faith and in the knowledge of the Son of God
and become mature . . .' (Eph 4:11–13). The word 'to
equip' is a fascinating word in the New Testament. It was
used of the disciples mending their nets after a night's
fishing. We can imagine Peter and John untangling the
nets, mending any parts that had broken, throwing out
weed and flotsam caught in the nets, in order that they
could use the nets again. The Lord has provided the
scriptures, his servants and his Spirit (2 Tim 3:16–17; Eph
4:11; 2 Cor 1:22) so that we can be like repaired nets – ready
for the Lord to use. This reminds us, clearly, that the third
function of his body *is to be involved in mission*. The church
should be made up of shepherds and fishermen, to tend the
flock and to land the fish. The church as the body of Christ is
to use both the hook and the crook!

## We must value the membership of the church

It is one thing to understand what the church is and what it
is for. It is another matter, completely, to have a truly

biblical understanding of church membership. Churches in different countries and of different denominations have different domestic rules and standards as to what constitutes membership. For example, a church such as 'The Church on the Way' in California, which is pastored by Jack Hayford, states clearly that membership requires that you:

1. Have received Jesus Christ as your Saviour (Jn 3:3–5).
2. Agree with the church's statement of faith.
3. Will support the congregation's ministry with tithes, offerings and intercessory prayer.
4. Want to serve the Lord Jesus and will wait on Him to disclose to you your place of ministry in the ongoing life of our fellowship.[2]

Membership has both privileges and responsibilities in the body of Christ.

By contrast, an official member of the Church of England is any lay person entitled to have his name entered on the electoral roll of the parish if he can satisfy certain conditions. They are that he is baptised, a member of the Church of England or of a church in communion with the Church of England, is seventeen years or upwards, is resident in the parish, or if not so resident, has habitually attended public worship in the parish during the period of six months prior to enrolment and has signed the form of application for enrolment.[3] These conditions can be read in such a way that one thinks this is all that being a member of the body of Christ implies. To be honest and realistic, there are many on our membership rolls who have not fully understood what membership of the church means. The result has been nominal membership rather than committed membership.

It is not surprising that many individual Anglican churches not only have their electoral roll, which is the legal record of membership qualified to vote at the annual church meeting, but also prepare their own congregational membership lists. We are all beginning to take church membership more seriously, but there is still a long way to go.

The true biblical standard of membership is of those who

are in Christ, who accept the fundamental creeds of the Christian church, who understand that their conduct is to be 'as Christ', and who are willing to commit themselves wholly to one another and to the Lord.

Sadly, this is the exception rather than the rule. Church members have been described as billiard balls who bounce off one another, or as never being willing for the outward mask to be penetrated and the real person discovered. Keith Miller has written:

> Our churches are filled with people who outwardly look contented and at peace but inwardly are crying out for someone to love them . . . just as they are – confused, frustrated, often frightened, guilty, and often unable to communicate even within their own families. But the *other* people in the church *look* so happy and contented that one seldom has the courage to admit his own deep needs before such a self-sufficient group as the average church meeting appears to be.[4]

One such apparently self-sufficient church member was Peter, yet Jesus knew he was hurting inside, and brought him to the point where he would acknowledge both his failure and his need, and then in a display of supernatural grace trusted him with one of the most important jobs in the world (Jn 21:17). Instead of Peter believing that he was useless, Jesus made him useful; our Lord and master is always taking broken people, and misshapen clay, and moulding them into some lovely members of his body.

## We must understand about ministry and gifts

Some people see themselves as *supporters* of the church – rather like the buttresses of the building. They take the church magazine, attend on high days and festivals and give the 'generous' donation of £10 a year! Others see themselves as church *attenders*, and unless they are away on holiday or prevented by illness will be in their traditional place every Sunday – thank God for such. But the *true church member* is like the pillar of a church – that which really supports and maintains the work of the church. They are those who will be busy in one of many ways – welcoming people, doing the flowers, ministering to the sick, serving meals, delivering the newsletter or helping out in the Sunday school. Paul tells us that when every part is working properly the body grows and builds itself up in love (Eph 4:16).

For many people, however, there is the difficulty of knowing what the Lord wants them to be doing within the church by way of service. The answer to that very real problem lies in understanding what the New Testament teaches about the ministry of the church and the gifts of the Spirit.

The New Testament has various lists of ministries and gifts. The key passages are found in Romans 12, Ephesians 4, 1 Corinthians 12 and 14, and 1 Peter 4. In those passages different Greek words are used to describe the working of God's Spirit. For example: there is a *charismatos* – a gift of grace (Rom 12:3–8); a *phanerosis* – a ministry of the Spirit (1 Cor 12:7) and *domata* – gifts to equip men (Eph 4:8).

It is helpful to note that the three persons of the Trinity – the Father, the Son and the Holy Spirit – are active within the ministry and 'gifting' of the church. It is also essential that we spell out some distinctions implicit within the gifts and ministries, in order to dispel a great deal of confusion.

*The gifts of the Spirit are distinguishable from the gift of the Spirit.* If you study the example of Timothy in 2 Timothy 1:6, you will find that Timothy, like every Christian, had the gift of the Holy Spirit indwelling him. In addition Timothy had received certain gifts of the Spirit – probably the gift of teaching and the gift of the evangelist (2 Tim 4:2,5). Paul writes of the gifts of the Spirit in 1 Corinthians also. He stresses that these gifts will include tongues, the word of knowledge, of wisdom, the gifts of healing, etc (1 Cor 12:8–10). But he also emphasises that God in his sovereignty releases some of these gifts to every Christian as he wills (1 Cor 12:11). Thus every Christian has the gift of the Spirit, and every Christian has one or more of the gifts of the Spirit.

*The gifts of the Spirit and the fruit of the Spirit are distinguishable*. The gifts are the means by which the Lord of the church works – his conduct – while the fruit is the means by which Christ expresses his character. The gifts reflect what Christ does, the fruit what Christ is like. Each Christian will display some of the gifts, while each Christian should be producing all the fruit. The gifts may be demonstrated at once, the fruit will grow gradually.

*We must distinguish between the natural abilities that a Christian has, and the spiritual gifts and ministries that the Lord gives*. There is often a close link, in that the natural abilities become the seed-bed from which the spiritual gifts grow, but they are not the same.

*We may also distinguish between gifts, ministries and offices*. God may well release a word of prophecy to someone in the congregation once or twice. Should that continue, the church may well recognise that God is giving that person the ministry of the prophet within that church. Such a ministry might be officially recognised, so that the person holds a particular 'office' in the church, but this is not always so. Again, while every Christian is called to be a witness for Christ, and to testify to their faith, some Christians will discover they have been given the gift of the evangelist – they have a 'natural' way of sharing the faith with unconverted friends that God uses. The gift of evangelism could develop into the ministry of the evangelist, and if this is recognised officially by the church, they might be appointed to the office of an evangelist. So gifts can become ministries; and those who are called to ministry should be exercising the gifts that God has given to them.

*We can distinguish giving from liberality*. While every Christian is called to give, some will be in a position –

perhaps through inherited wealth or being a successful businessman – whereby they can exercise the gift of liberality, and release great financial resources for the body of Christ.

In a way, the gifts and ministries of the body of Christ are like the many varied electrical appliances we all have at home. They each do a different job; some are used more often than others, some are items we already had, and some have been given, but they all need to be plugged into the same central power supply to be used. In the case of the gifts and ministries that central supply is the resurrection power of God. In summary, we can say:

Spiritual gifts are abilities inspired by the Holy Spirit and reflecting Jesus Christ, which, while taking place within our human experience, nevertheless take us beyond our natural abilities into realms of which we are not humanly capable, in order that we may contribute significantly to the life and growth of the church and bring glory to God.[5]

For too long the church has tried to fulfil its calling without the gifts of the Spirit, and has been like a craftsman who does not know that the right tools for the job have been provided. When we are open to the gifts of the Spirit and discover our own ministry we shall be rejoicing in a new effectiveness for the Lord.

The difference has been put like this – 'maximum effectiveness and minimum weariness, instead of minimum effectiveness and maximum weariness'.

## We must find our place in the church

This is the crucial question in serving the Lord, and there are three different approaches we can take to find the answer.

The first is a very ad hoc method. You have been fulfilling a certain role for years because there was no one else to do the job. However, you have never really been sure that this was precisely the role that the Lord intended for you. It is all rather 'hit and miss'. The second way is to answer one of a number of questionnaires that are available.[6] In many respects both these ways can be very helpful, but I believe that we should also answer the question by a third approach: understanding and using the guidelines mentioned in the New Testament.

*Understand that every born-again Christian has at least one spiritual gift*. The New Testament writers in 1 Corinthians 12:7,11, Ephesians 4:16 and 1 Peter 4:10 all use the same word – 'each' or 'each one': there are no committed Christians without at least one spiritual gift or ministry given to them by Jesus.

*Prayerfully consider the possibilities*. We have already mentioned that we need to know what gifts are available. We also need to know ourselves and to have a sober estimate of ourselves. Many Christians lack self-confidence and they have a low view of their own worth. Some Christians have too exalted a view of themselves. The gifts will flow where we are able to have God's view of ourselves and think with a sober, balanced judgement.

The shy adult may feel that he or she is no use at all, but has the gift of ministering to children in a beautiful way. Others may believe they are not public speakers, and yet as they submit to the Lord and walk in the Spirit they are used by the Lord to bring the word of prophecy to the group and then they find the courage to speak out in the larger meeting. Someone else may realise that they love dealing with 'things' and are gifted administrators, other have a ministry of visiting and caring. Review the lists of the gifts mentioned in the New Testament and see where you fit in. They are rather like God's Job Centre where the un- or underemployed or wrongly employed can go to see what jobs are available in God's church.

*Allow others to judge the gifts you have*. Many of us find it difficult to be our own judges. We do not see all there is.

Other Christians can best discern the gifts and ministry we have. The small fellowship group or support group is very valuable in this way. If you belong to a fellowship group, I wonder whether you have ever read through the lists of the gifts and then helped one another discover and identify the gifts God has given you. It may be others who recognise more quickly and fully than we do that we have a gift of leading a group, or running a supper party, or visiting the lonely, etc. They will also lovingly tell us what gifts we do not have, and that is equally important.

*Desire to use your gift* (1 Cor 12:31; 14:1). Often we are like the servant with the one talent in the parable Jesus told (Mt 25:14–30, esp. v.25.) 'I was afraid and went out and hid your talent in the ground.' Fear, whether of failure or of stepping out in faith, is probably the main hindrance to many Christians. Hence the insistence that we must be willing to use the gifts that God has given to us. As we use those gifts – whether they be the gifts of faith or tongues, encouragement or hospitality – so the Lord will allow the gifts to develop and mature and become more fruitful. If we refuse to use what gifts we have, they will atrophy and die and we shall be like the branch in John 15 that brings forth no fruit. That branch is gathered up and put on the bonfire – it is an unfruitful branch. We must desire to use the gifts. We must not open a museum of the gifts that the risen Lord has given to us for others to see.

*Walk in the Spirit.* The gifts are given in the context of right and loving relationships with one another. Every passage devoted to the gifts of the Spirit also stresses the love of the fellowship as the right context in which those gifts can best operate. In that atmosphere of accepting love the young Christians will be able to take the first steps of faith in using their gifts. If love is one common link in the passages, faith is another. We are to use our gifts according to the measure of faith that God has given to us, so step out in love towards others and faith towards the Lord.

*Test the gifts.* We are told in 1 Thessalonians 5:21 to 'test everything' – that may mean the same thing as weighing prophecy in 1 Corinthians 14:29, where the church is called upon to assess and judge whether what is said by man is also said by God. The gift of prophecy is to be tested in that very special way, but all gifts are to be tested. If we have tried something that is not God's ministry for us, then we are not to worry, God has something else.

Peter Wagner tells what a relief it was to discover that he had not been given the gift of the evangelist, because he had not been successful and blessed in that; rather God was calling him to the ministry of a teacher and pastor.[7]

Dr Wagner has spent much time in the study of spiritual gifts. He has written of his conclusions as follows:

> My studies of the growing churches in America have not led me to believe that the question of which spiritual gifts are or are not now in effect is a primary growth factor. Much more important seems to be the recognition that the Holy Spirit is working through gifts and that Christians need to discover, develop and use them.[8]

## We must begin to use every-member ministry

The one-man band does not turn overnight into the body working properly. Our experience is that in many churches there is some attempt to involve other members of the church in ministry. If there are blockages, they may equally well be on the part of the members ('He's paid to do the job') as well as the minister who is so filled with fear or pride that he will allow nothing to happen unless he is present. Again, our experience is that most changes come about in church by means of evolution rather than revolution. It is a gradual process. Yet there are some basic facts which must operate if a fellowship is to encourage every member to find their role and serve the Lord.

There must be the right understanding. We have to understand what the New Testament is teaching about

ministry, the purpose of the church, and nature of the gifts
and how I discover what mine are. In other words, there
will have to be patient and persistent teaching of the kind of
material I have already dealt with in this chapter. While it
may be familiar to some, it will be new – and revolutionary
– to others. It is better to teach the same thing two or three
times, rather than assuming that a congregation knows and
understands. For example, in our church we had spoken –
and used – the gift of words of knowledge in the Sunday
services, but it was not until I had taught about them in a
sermon, and then asked the Holy Spirit to release them
within the congregation, that quite a number of members
realised what was meant by them. Teaching removed both
the ignorance and the mystery in many minds.

There must be the right opportunity to use the gifts and
for people to minister. This is a practical and local issue. It
will concern the policy of the church. Can the gifts in 1
Corinthians 12 be used within the main worship services –
and if so, how will that be controlled? May all the gifts and
ministries be exercised within small fellowship groups in
the church? How shall we look out for new workers?
How can we help the members of the church to discover
their role? Should there be a regular series of talks for
newcomers to the church so that they can understand the
working philosophy of the church, discover their part in the
church, and feel they really belong? All these are matters of
local decision by the leadership, but the right opportunities
must be given to the members.

There also needs to be the right attitude and spirit in the
church for the flowering of ministries and gifts. There will
be attitudes to avoid, and attitudes to encourage. For
example, in 1 Corinthians 12:15–26 Paul tells the Corinthians to avoid the attitude that says 'I'm not needed.' We
must not make others in the fellowship feel that they are
inferior and do not matter. On the other hand there must
not be the superior outlook that suggests we are more
important than others. Rather, there should be the sense
that we belong and we are mutually responsible to and for
each other, that we are members one of another, and that

we care for, honour and suffer with one another. One way to create these right attitudes – instead of inferiority or superiority – is to stress the New Testament idea 'stewardship' (1 Pet 4:10). All have been given a gift and a task by the Lord. It comes from him, and we are to use that gift for one another and for his glory.

We shall also need to allow one another to grow in faith, to make mistakes and not get laughed at or criticised. In many ways, the church is the Lord's apprentice school. We are discovering, in our own church, how to give one another room to learn. For example, we all have to speak out for the first time in words of knowledge or prophecy. How do you make a start? A little phrase like, 'I'm not sure, but I think the Lord is saying . . .' or, 'I keep seeing a picture of', or 'The word "discouragement" keeps coming to me' all allow us to learn together. We trust together, we love together and we laugh together. The body is beginning to work as it should. Or someone may feel they are called to help lead a group, or care for the bereaved, or face the challenge of missionary service. In every case we need to show the person the next step to test that calling, and not to worry if they haven't heard the Lord exactly right. Such an attitude needs the spirit of love and acceptance, of faith and of obedience. But it is in that atmosphere that we can best begin to use the gifts and exercise our ministry.

## We must mobilise and train the members

'Christ has no body on earth but yours. No hands but yours. No feet but yours. Yours are the eyes through which Christ's compassion looks out on the world, yours are the feet with which he goes about doing good, yours are the hands with which he is to bless us now.' St Teresa of Avila's prayer sums up what serving the Lord is all about. We may know the theory, but how do we get the show on the road! Administry, in a report entitled *Just the Job*, surveyed over one hundred churches to ask questions about mobilising their members: '85% of the churches surveyed say they have too few labourers; 72% a shortage in "leadership" roles, 54% in "practical" roles; 57% have members dangerously overworked; and 92% do not find most of their members willingly using gifts/skills.'[9] A not uncommon situation! What can be done to unblock this, and mobilise and train the members? I think there are four issues we need to consider.

*There is the need to motivate people*. Why are we or they doing this? Am I working because of the human call of the church, the need of the work, the reputation before others, the satisfaction I personally derive, or am I called to this? To use Gordon Macdonald's question: 'Am I called or am I driven?' Driven by men or called by God? When our lives are transformed by the gospel and open to the Spirit and we have discovered what the Lord wants us to do, then we shall begin to find that 'His service is perfect freedom.'

*There is the need to mobilise the people*. The Administry report to which I have referred poses four questions that every church needs to consider if it would fully and happily mobilise the congregation. a) Is there a wide enough leadership base responsible to find, inspire and appoint the workers? For example, who is responsible to find the new Sunday school teacher, the magazine editor, the helper with the cubs, the person to run the prayer chain, etc? Every church will have its own answer. It may be the minister, it may be a group of leaders, it may be a senior leader or head of department. Whatever the answer it needs to be clear, and it needs to be known. b) How are people made aware of the needs of the work? For example, is there good communication within the church, or are the leaders complaining that no one is coming forward, when in fact they haven't communicated the real needs to all the members? c) How can you help people realise they can do the job? All of us need encouragement as well as a clear understanding of what the job requires and how long we are expected to do it – or are all appointments 'for life', or 'till death, boredom or breakdown do us part'? d) How do you set about involving every member of the church? Few churches seem to have done this successfully, and most need to understand that to be done properly it must be taken seriously and regarded as a long-term project, and not a flash in the pan or the minister's latest idea!

*There is the need to model the ministry*. Just as the disciples spent three years with Jesus and saw how he 'modelled the ministry', so do we. After all, Peter would not have known how to raise someone from the dead unless he had first seen Jesus do it (Acts 9:36–41; cf. Mk 5:35–43)! Paul did the same thing with men like Timothy and Silas. Programmes such as Evangelism Explosion, and Teach and Reach, or Fellowships like the Vineyard Christian Ministries, have all been blessed and grown in fruitfulness because they have not just taught with words, they have enabled people to see and to do. We have many opportunities to model the ministry in our local churches which we don't always take – younger people sitting in with experienced Sunday School teachers, potential group leaders sharing with older Bible study or nurture group leaders, the investment by the minister or pastor of his time and himself with his key lay leaders so that he is enabled to give away his ministry and have it reproduced in others, taking people with us on visits to other fellowships and churches and getting them involved in one-off situations. People are thrilled to know they can 'do it' and that the Lord will use them, and they are eager for more.

*There is the need to maintain the vision and sense of direction of the church*. Our church's purpose is summed up in the phrase, which is not unique, 'To know Christ and to make him known.' We have to spend time helping people understand what this means in practice and sharing the vision of the church. Leaders and members alike need to 'own' one another. We need also to have realistic short-term goals so that the whole body, or a particular part of the body, is able to measure how it is getting on. We shall need to have the proper escape routes for members who, finding their circumstances have changed, need to amend their role in the church without feeling that they have let others down or that they have to 'hang in there' until exhaustion or 'burnout' forces them to give way.

## We must emphasise the importance of love

Whenever gifts, ministry and serving the Lord together are mentioned in those four key New Testament passages (Rom 12; 1 Cor 12; Eph 4; 1 Pet 4) love is also mentioned. The love of Christ calls us to serve him, and the love which the Spirit of Christ gives to his body is the atmosphere in which we find the freedom to serve. Of course Satan wants it to be otherwise, and he tries to stir up disunity, provoke criticism and misunderstanding and create doubt and despair so that the work the Lord has called us to is not done. But love will ultimately triumph.

That marvellous hymn to love in 1 Corinthians 13 is often taken right out of its natural setting. It comes between 1 Corinthians 12 and 14, which talk about tension over the use of the gifts. Paul shows that where love operates the body will build itself up. A loving fellowship should be like a dry-dock where the church is made ready and equipped for its mission; it should be like the port from which it goes forth into the world, and like the harbour where its members can return and find shelter and refuge from the battle. Such a harbour and port will have the flags of love flying from the mast head. Such love will also be very practical and personal.

It will be love that is both forgiving and forgiven. The church will be a place where people can confess their needs and sins and failures and find understanding and acceptance. It will be love that encourages and affirms one another rather than rivals and criticises. It will be love that is humble and lowly, willing to do the smallest and most menial task, and ready to overlook the largest hurt that others may have given. There will be an openness to one another, so that we no longer have to hide behind masks of respectability, but can be free to allow other Christians to see the real 'us' and not feel vulnerable. It will be love that gives and doesn't take, love that welcomes and does not reject, love that supports and prays for each other, love that trusts and is not fearful. Such love is not human love, but the love of God shed abroad in our hearts by the Holy Spirit. It will be the love that Jesus displayed as he modelled for his disciples what it meant to be a servant of all.

John tells us that Jesus, having loved his own who were in the world, now showed his disciples the full extent of his love. He was the Son of God. He had come from heaven and he was going to heaven. Yet what an example we are given in Jn 13:4–5. Using six short action verbs, John describes how Jesus demonstrated Christian service for all time. He got up from the meal, took off his outer clothing, wrapped a towel around his waist, poured water into a basin, began to wash his disciples' feet, and wiped them with a towel. He became the house slave to his disciples, although he was truly the Son of God.

If the church throughout the world truly wants to demonstrate the lordship of Jesus today, it must use the gifts the Lord has given, live in the love the Lord has shown, and possess the humility of mind and spirit the Lord displayed. In that way we shall not only enter fully into the joy of service and the fruitfulness of Christian ministry, but we shall be showing in a very practical way what it means both individually and corporately to serve the Lord in the fellowship of his church and in the power of His Spirit.

## For personal reflection or group study

1 Do you believe you have found your place in the body of Christ?
2 How were you helped to do this?
3 What do you think would have been more helpful to this end?

# 8 THE SPIRIT OF THE LORD

Sir Henry Cole (no relation) was responsible for distributing the first printed Christmas cards. In 1846 he decided to send them to his friends, and the custom has continued to this day.

Who is it, however, who first sent circular letters to his friends at Christmas with all the family and church news of the last twelve months? (St Paul, perhaps?). Such a habit has been growing among Christians, and it was in one such letter that a friend wrote to me about the recent events at his church.

> We had a combined committee meeting a week ago to consider 'mission' and 'growth'. It ended up more like 'groans' than 'growth'. Looking back one wonders how twenty or so mature Christians can talk for two hours and get nowhere! About the only thing we did eventually agree on was to take the doors off the pews – and do it with a flourish and the press present as a symbolic act to mark our opening up to others. It was also suggested we say 'Amen' more loudly. Oh yes, and we agreed to meet again in February.

Sadly, others will be familiar with such experiences. What a contrast with the life of the early church as recorded in Acts.

This is an account of the church praying and preaching, travelling and teaching. A small group of men and women dedicated to the Lord and driven on by the Holy Spirit. Luke the historian records the establishment of the church at Jerusalem and the preaching of Peter, then the spread of Christianity through Palestine and into Samaria. There is the martyrdom of Stephen and the conversion of Saul. The gospel comes to Antioch, Cornelius is converted and the

Gentiles receive the gospel. The flame and fire of the gospel of Jesus spreads into Asia Minor and then into Europe with the missionary journeys of Paul and his companions to the great cities of Corinth, Ephesus, Athens and Rome. It is often said that the Acts of the Apostles should be called the Acts of the Holy Spirit, and that is true, yet the one who is mentioned most often is the Lord Jesus. There are something like 180 different references to the Lord Jesus, while there are only about seventy references to the Holy Spirit. This demonstrates to us that where Jesus is Lord the Holy Spirit is at work, and where the Holy Spirit is at work then Jesus will be Lord.

Today, sadly, many Christians are living sub-normal lives, so that we have come to accept the sub-normal as normal. What the New Testament is teaching is that the normal Christian life is one that acknowledges that Jesus is Lord, and experiences the continual ministry and power of the Spirit.

As David Watson has written:

Take him away, and you have no church: an institution, an organisation, a building, a structure, perhaps; but no church of the living God. Yet Dr. Carl Bates once commented, 'If God were to take the Holy Spirit out of our midst today, about 95 per cent of what we are doing in our churches would go on, and we would not know the difference.'[1]

The testimony of the New Testament is that we know more about the Spirit of the Lord as we acknowledge the lordship of Christ. We find this to be true in the teaching of the New Testament, in the history of the early church, and also in the ministry of Jesus himself. I want to look at each of these in turn, and then show how churches and Christians can discover more about the reality and ministry of the Spirit in their own lives today.

# The ministry of Jesus himself

We must not fall into the trap of thinking that the Holy Spirit began to make his appearance on the pages of scripture with the ministry of Jesus. He was there with the Father and the Son before the beginning of creation. As Genesis 1:2 records, 'The Spirit of God was hovering over the waters.' The Bible is like a three-act play. In Act One, God the Father is the chief character on the stage of the Old Testament, with the Son and the Spirit off-stage in the wings, making the occasional appearance. Act Two reveals the ministry of Jesus upon earth, with Jesus himself centre-stage, and with the Father and the Spirit making appearances. Act Three began with the coming of the Spirit at Pentecost and the birth of the church. The Holy Spirit – as we have seen with the summary of the events in the Acts – is in the spotlight. God has not withdrawn his Spirit or changed his plans.

In the Old Testament, the Spirit is revealed as the Spirit active in creation (Gen 1:2; Ps 33:6; 104:30); he endowed men like Gideon and Samson with power for special occasions. He bestowed natural creative gifts on some, and supernatural gifts of prophecy and wisdom on others (Exod 35:30–36:1; Num 11:16–17; 24:2; Judg 6:34; 14:6; 1 Kings 3:4–15).

Above all, the Holy Spirit is spoken of as the promised Spirit whom God will pour out upon all people, and his coming will be the sign of the new covenant (Jer 31:31–34; Ezek 36:25–27). When Jesus came, his life and ministry were enabled by the power of the Spirit. When Mary was told by the angel Gabriel that she would have a child, while still a virgin, she asked the obvious question – 'How will this be?', to which the angel replied, 'The Holy Spirit will come upon you, and the power of the Most High will overshadow you. So the holy one to be born will be called the Son of God' (Lk 1:34–35). Jesus was 'conceived of the Holy Spirit and born of the Virgin Mary'.

When Jesus was baptised by John the Holy Spirit descended upon him in bodily form like a dove (Lk 3:21–22) and then, full of the Holy Spirit, Jesus was driven into the desert to be tempted by Satan. Jesus' ministry was anointed by the Spirit of God: 'The Spirit of the Lord is on me, because he has anointed me to preach good news to the poor. He has sent me to proclaim freedom for the prisoners and recovery of sight for the blind, to release the oppressed, to proclaim the year of the Lord's favour' (Lk 4:18–19). Jesus began and continued his ministry in the power and inspiration of the Holy Spirit.

Jesus is also the baptiser with the Holy Spirit. As Michael Green has written: 'You cannot get the Holy Spirit except through Jesus, or get to Jesus except through the Holy Spirit.'[2]

I suppose there is no phrase that causes as much confusion in the Christian church today as 'the baptism of the Spirit'. What is clear is that there is such a spiritual reality as the baptism of the Spirit. Surely John the Baptist would not point a way to Jesus as the Lamb of God who takes away the sin of the world (Jn 1:29), and as the one 'who will baptise with the Holy Spirit' (Jn 1:33), if we were not able to experience both forgiveness through the atonement and power through the baptism of the Spirit. What is clear is that Luke, so accurate and precise in his historical investigation for his gospel and Acts, appears to be theologically imprecise about this baptism. At the end of his gospel and at the beginning of the history of the early church he happily uses a variety of terms to describe the same event. He reports Jesus saying to the disciples, 'I am going to send you what my Father has promised; but stay in the city until you are clothed with power from on high' (Lk 24:49). Later, referring to the same event in the Acts, Luke writes: 'Do not leave Jerusalem, but wait for the gift my Father promised, which you have heard me speak about. For John baptised with water, but in a few days you will be baptised with the Holy Spirit . . . you will receive power when the Holy Spirit comes on you; and you will be my witnesses . . .' (Acts 1:4–5,8). And writing of Pentecost itself, Luke records, 'All of them were filled with the Holy Spirit and began to speak in other tongues as the Spirit enabled them'

(Acts 2:4). Speaking of the same event, Jesus and Luke described it as a baptism, a filling, an anointing with power, the promise of the Father, and being clothed with power from on high.

Jesus came in the power of the Spirit, and he promised to baptise his disciples in the Spirit for their ministry. He also spent time teaching them more about the Holy Spirit during his final days upon earth (Jn 14–16). He taught them that the Spirit is someone just like himself who will be with us for ever, and whose ministry is to convict the world of its unbelief; who will bring new life to men and women; who will teach the disciples; who will bear witness to Jesus and enable the church to glorify the Lord.

It is quite clear that the church is not able to fulfil its mission in the world apart from the presence and power of the person of the Holy Spirit.


## The history of the early church

The accounts of the early church show us that they had grasped this truth and knew its reality. For example, Peter and John were involved in a ministry of 'signs and wonders' as they met at the Beautiful Gate the man who was lame from birth and whom Peter healed in the name of Jesus. Not surprisingly an excited crowd quickly gathered, and Peter lost no time in preaching the gospel. The religious authorities arrested the disciples, interrogated them and after a night in prison released them with a solemn warning that such behaviour and witness would not be tolerated again. In spite of this threat the disciples went back to their friends and held a praise and prayer meeting before setting out again to witness to the risen Christ.

In his account of the events, Luke makes it very clear that while the apostles gave praise to the Father and sovereign Lord who had made the earth, they preached and witnessed in the name of Jesus, and that they were able to do this in the power or fullness of the Spirit. In fact we find that when the Holy Spirit is given to the church on the day of

Pentecost, as promised, the ministries of the Spirit are released, the fruit of the Spirit is displayed in their lives, and the life of the church is revolutionised.

Any superficial reading of the early chapters of Acts will show that the fellowship was deep and real. It involved community living and financial sharing. There was constant prayer and praise. There was a reality in their worship which they had never known before. The earliest disciples were led by the Spirit not only to a sharing of possessions but also to a tremendous depth of worship. The Spirit, and not the church or the apostles, initiated and drove them out in mission, and inspired within them their burning desire for holiness of life and their active involvement in the ministry of the body.

## The teaching of the New Testament

In various ways the New Testament states that you cannot know Jesus without knowing the Spirit and vice versa. The first Christian confession, as stated in 1 Corinthians 12:3, is possible only through the Holy Spirit: 'No one can say, "Jesus is Lord," except by the Holy Spirit.' Having the Spirit is the distinctive mark of being a Christian: 'And if anyone does not have the Spirit of Christ, he does not belong to Christ' (Rom 8:9). The early preaching at Pentecost made the same claim:

> Peter replied, 'Repent and be baptised, every one of you, in the name of Jesus Christ for the forgiveness of your sins. And you will receive the gift of the Holy Spirit. The promise is for you and your children and for all who are far off – for all whom the Lord our God will call.'
>
> (Acts 2:38–39)

The letter to the Ephesians, which teaches so clearly the lordship of Jesus over his church as his body, is also the letter that teaches so much about the ministry of the Holy Spirit. Jesus is portrayed as the Lord from creation, through the cross, over the church, within the community, and in the conflict with Satan (Eph 1:4–10; 2:14–18; 4:1–16; 5:21–6:9; 6:10–18). At the same time, Paul teaches about the Holy Spirit:

*He seals the believers* (Eph 1:13–14). The picture here is of a seal that is like an engagement ring or a down payment on something. It is the legal assurance that we belong to the Lord and that there is much more to follow.

*He makes the presence of God real* (Eph 2:22). The church is called to be the temple, or the dwelling, of God. The Greek word used is *naos*, which means the sanctuary into which only the priests in the Old Testament could go. Paul wants to stress the contrast between the distance and separation from God maintained under the old covenant and the intimacy we are invited to have with the Lord under the new covenant. It is the work of the Holy Spirit to bring us into 'whispering distance' with the Lord.

*He strengthens the Christians for the work of God.* Paul has already prayed that every believer at Ephesus might know the incomparably great power of God at work in us who believe, and that they might be strengthened with power through the Spirit in their inner being (Eph 1:19; 3:16).

Later on, he speaks about the Lord who is able to do immeasurably more than all we ask or imagine, according to his power that is at work in us (Eph 3:20–21). If we ask what hinders the working of the Spirit, Paul gives us some of the answers in the same letter, for the Spirit is also . . .

*The spirit of unity* (Eph 4:3). 'Be completely humble and gentle; be patient, bearing with one another in love. Make every effort to keep the unity of the Spirit through the bond of peace. There is one body and one Spirit' (Eph 4:2–4). Where Christians are divided or just out of touch with each other, we shall to that same extent limit the power of the Spirit. Where there is criticism, grumbling and division which denies the lordship of Jesus over his church, so there will be a limit to the power of the Spirit.

Surely it is remarkable that, through the renewing work of the Spirit, Christians who previously were out of fellowship with one another have come to acknowledge the lordship of Jesus and the power of the Spirit in a new way. Protestant and Catholic, black and white, have bowed the knee to Jesus and at the same time known divisions have melted away through the work of the Spirit. The renewing work of the Spirit within his church is the true and lasting ecumenical movement that today's world needs. It is one thing for men to make policy decisions – and they are important – it is another for the Spirit of God to change the hearts of men and women – and that is essential.

*The Spirit of holiness* (Eph 4:30). Paul has been writing about our speech and our reactions, our work and our anger, our attitude to money and our giving to others. Into the middle of these very down-to-earth instructions, he tells the Christians not to grieve the Holy Spirit, with whom they were sealed for the day of redemption. We can grieve the Holy Spirit in very simple and practical ways. Thus, again, our availability to the Holy Spirit will depend upon the lordship of Jesus over our minds and mouths, our marriages and money.

*The fullness of the Spirit* (Eph 5:18). It is with a sense of humour that Paul contrasts the effects of drink and the effects of the Spirit of Jesus. The man or woman who has had too much to drink will be unsteady on their feet, slurred in their speech, confused in their thinking and loud-mouthed in their singing. Every Christian is to permit the Spirit to influence their living and thinking, talking and singing. The apostle's command literally means in the Greek, 'All of you must allow the Holy Spirit to go on filling you.' As has been said, there is one baptism, many fillings and a constant anointing by the Holy Spirit.

## The Spirit and the church

The Church throughout the world today is rediscovering these truths, and is experiencing the ministries and gifts of the Holy Spirit. It is also learning to keep the balance between the fruit of the Spirit and the gifts of the Spirit, and to see that both become effective when Jesus is acknowledged as the Lord.

The Spirit alone will produce the fruit of love, joy, peace, patience, kindness, goodness, faithfulness, gentleness and self-control; but such fruit will only appear as each believer is abiding in Christ. Obedience and submission may be old-fashioned and unpopular words for today, but they are the key to knowing the Spirit's work and character.

We have already noted that Paul in 1 Corinthians 12 began his teaching about the gifts of the Spirit – such as prophecy, healing, tongues, discernment, etc. – by establishing the lordship of Jesus.

Perhaps the clearest link between the gifts of the Spirit and the lordship of Jesus comes in Romans 12. Paul has set out the account of God's mercy to sinners, and now he makes his appeal: 'Therefore, I urge you, brothers, in view of God's mercy, to offer your bodies as living sacrifices, holy and pleasing to God – this is your spiritual act of worship. Do not conform any longer to the pattern of this world, but be transformed by the renewing of your mind. Then you will be able to test and approve what God's will is – his good, pleasing and perfect will' (Rom 12:1–2). Most of us stop at that point. It's the end of a paragraph and Paul seems to be going on to a new subject. But that is not so. Paul is actually continuing the theme. He now comes to a very practical stage in the application: 'For by the grace given me I say to every one of you . . .' and he goes on to speak about every Christian in the church using the gifts of teaching, encouragement, administration, counsel, etc. that God has given to them. We shall know the gifts and ministries of the Spirit as we yield to the lordship of Jesus.

Paul uses the most helpful Old Testament picture of sacrifice. Some sacrifices were to be offered for sin. Others, including the whole burnt offering, which he has in mind here, were to be offered up as a demonstration of fellowship and love and joy.

The burnt offering was to be offered up as a clean offering, as a complete offering (every part was to be presented to God) and as a continual offering – day and night, high days and holidays. In the same way the Christian is called to constantly offer his life, clean and holy to God; he is to offer up every part – mind, body, heart, emotions, abilities, etc. – to the Lord, and the result will be the discovery and use of the gifts of service imparted by the Spirit. But why does the church not always demonstrate this power of the Spirit, which Christ knew and the early church rejoiced in? If there is one word more than any other that sums up why we do not know this same dynamic power of the Spirit today it must be 'fear'. At first sight this may not appear to be the root cause. We are held back by tradition, disobedience, unbelief, ignorance and worldliness, but behind much of this will be fear.

It is fear that keeps so many churches from this dynamic life – the fear of allowing the Lord Jesus to have control, the fear of being open to all that the Holy Spirit wishes to do. It is not surprising, therefore, that Paul twice has to reassure the Christians that the Spirit they have been given is not the Spirit of fear (Rom 8:15; 2 Tim 1:7). It is significant that the first act the risen Christ performed among the disciples was to dispel the spirit of fear and speak his peace to them. Then he reminded them of their mission and released to them his power (Jn 20:19–23). The same is still true today.

One of the most fearless Christians I know is Canon James Wong from Singapore. He is a key figure in the renewal of the church in South East Asia, and a pioneer in church growth. Through his work – and that of many others – God has been bringing very significant growth to the young church in Singapore. They have much to teach other parts of the world, and they also have a right to comment on other parts of the world. When Canon Wong visited Britain in 1985 he was asked about the church in different parts of the world.

When I go to Thailand I expect to be confronted by the Buddhist way of life. When I go to India I expect to see shrines to Hinduism. When I go to Moslem countries I expect to make a cultural adjustment to Islam. When I come to Britain, I don't expect to see living, dynamic believing Christians. I expect to see a materialistic, secularist, hedonistic society. I don't think of Britain as a Christian nation. I have seen a lot of churches here, but they are old dead monuments and I am not impressed by them. At the same time, wherever churches are open to the Holy Spirit, wherever the Word of God is faithfully proclaimed and preached, wherever there is vital worship and loving personal relationships there a church is built up. The Gospel has power to change things and I have visited some very lively churches in Britain where I have seen the power of God at work. They are the spiritual lighthouses.[3]

## Knowing the power of the Spirit

It is through our relationship with the Father and the Son that we receive the fullness of the Spirit.

I find the acrostic 'total' a very useful word upon which to hang the biblical instructions for knowing the ministry and power of the Spirit. It brings together in logical order the believer's response to the Father and the Son if he is to know the fullness of the Spirit's power.

*We must turn and repent* of any sin and hindrance, disobedience and unbelief that is in our lives if we are to know the power of the Spirit. As Peter puts it in his sermon 'Repent, then, and turn to God, so that your sins may be wiped out, that times of refreshment may come from the Lord . . .' (Acts 3:19). Repentance, in the Bible, is always turning away from sin and turning towards God. When David was convicted of his sinful relationship to Bathsheba, he confessed and repented before God himself, and prayed that the Lord would renew a steadfast spirit within him, rather than taking the Holy Spirit from him (Ps 51:10–11).

Many a Christian has discovered that the way into greater power is through repentance of known sin. As we repent of the areas of bitterness and resentment locked away in our lives, so we shall experience a fresh outpouring of the Spirit. Repentance is, in fact, the key to renewal.

*We must obey God.* It is Peter again, speaking in Acts 5:32, who says, 'We are witnesses of these things, and so is the Holy Spirit, whom God has given to those who obey him.' Since the Spirit of God is the *Holy* Spirit, we shall frustrate his purposes and quench his power if we disobey what the Spirit is saying to us. It is significant that Acts 5 begins with the dramatic account of Ananias and Sapphira selling their land and then bringing only part of the purchase price (although claiming it to be the total price) to the apostles. There were remarkable and fatal results. Before they die, Peter examines them both and says, 'How is it that Satan has so filled your heart that you have lied to the Holy Spirit and have kept for yourself some of the money you received for the land? . . . How could you agree to test the Spirit of the Lord?' (Acts 5:3,9). As they disobeyed the Spirit, so they drastically limited what he would do.

The same point was made by the Bishop of Peru, Bishop David Evans, speaking on the great missionary commission at an international conference. Referring to Jesus' promise and purpose at the end of Matthew 28 ('Go ye therefore . . . and, lo, I am with you alway . . .' (AV)), Bishop Evans said, 'If there is no "Go", there will be no "Lo".' No obedience, no power.

God brought this same point before us as a congregation. We had set aside a long weekend between Ascension Day and the following Sunday for prayer. There was much that we could do within the church and parish. We had been challenged about church growth, about evangelism, and about our concern for young people in the parish who had only the pubs to go to for their social meetings; we were also beginning to discover new things in worship, and we longed to move forward. At the same time, we were seeking to complete a one hundred percent increase in our giving over a two year period. We wanted to ask the Lord to show us his vision, and to release among us his provision of money and people.

As we prayed and asked his blessing, one person present was given – in prayer – the picture of a beautifully iced wedding cake. Outwardly it looked good. Then a cross section of the cake revealed that inside the cake parts were going mouldy – and no good cake will go bad, especially if it is a rich fruit cake with wine or brandy in it. We asked the Lord what this picture meant and two people quite independently of each other had the word 'disobedience'.

We needed as a congregation, just as any individual Christian needs, to search our hearts to know if there were areas of disobedience that were restricting the power of the Spirit by not honouring the lordship of Jesus in every aspect.

No hymn better expresses these truths than that written by J. Edwin Orr, the great authority on revivals of the Holy Spirit in the world during the last fifty years:

Search me, O God, and know my heart today;
Try me, O Lord, and know my thoughts I pray:
See if there be some wicked way in me,
Cleanse me from ev'ry sin and set me free.

O Holy Ghost, revival comes from Thee;
Send a revival – start the work in me:
Thy Word declares Thou wilt supply our need;
For blessing now, O Lord, I humbly plead.[4]

*We must thirst for God.* Jesus made that abundantly clear when he said:

'If anyone is thirsty, let him come to me and drink. Whoever believes in me, as the Scripture has said, streams of living water will flow from within him.' By this

he meant the Spirit, whom those who believed in him
were later to receive. Up to that time the Spirit had not
been given, since Jesus had not yet been glorified.

(Jn 7:37–39)

Could anything be simpler or clearer? We need to come
to Jesus thirsty for more if we would receive more of the
Spirit. When we are thirsty and come to Jesus he goes on
giving us the refreshing supply of the Holy Spirit.

Praise God that more and more Christians are being
made 'thirsty' for more of the Lord and that as they long to
discover more of Jesus so he gives them more of his Spirit.
When Jesus was teaching his disciples for the first time
about the gift of the Spirit, whom only they – and not the
world – would be able to receive, he described the Spirit as
'another Counsellor' or 'Comforter' who would be with
them for ever (Jn 14:16). He tells them he will send them
someone just like himself. He will teach, guide, strengthen
and make himself known to each believer. Does not that
make you want to know him and find him? Are you not
beginning to become more and more thirsty for the Lord?
Then what do you have to do?

*We must ask for the Spirit*. Jesus tells us in Luke 11:13: 'If
you then, though you are evil, know how to give good gifts
to your children, how much more will your Father in
heaven give the Holy Spirit to those who ask Him!' God the
Father is no miserly orphanage-keeper who complains
when the Christian 'Oliver' comes along with an empty life
and asks for more!

We have worked our way through the first four steps of
entering into the greater power of the Holy Spirit through
the name of Jesus as we turn afresh to the Father. Each
Christian will be at a different point in the spiritual journey: some will need to turn and repent, all will need to
obey, each one will need to go on being thirsty, and
everyone will need to go on asking the Lord to give them of
his Spirit. But there is a fifth lesson.

*We must lean on God's word*. We all need to learn the lesson that Paul had to teach the Galatians. In one of the most frank and blunt passages in the New Testament, Paul asks them:

> O you dear idiots of Galatia, who saw Jesus Christ the crucified so plainly, who has been casting a spell over you? I will ask you one simple question: did you receive the Spirit by trying to keep the Law or by believing the message of the gospel? Surely you can't be so idiotic as to think that a man begins his spiritual life in the Spirit and then completes it by reverting to outward observances? Has all your painful experience brought you nowhere? I simply cannot believe it of you! Does God, who gives you his Spirit and works miracles among you, do these things because you have obeyed the Law or because you have believed the gospel? Ask yourselves that.[5]

We need to learn the lesson of relying upon, or leaning upon, the promise of the word of God about the gift of the Spirit – we need to learn to live by faith in his indwelling presence.

A group of Christians were praying one Friday evening, and God showed them a picture – through prayer – of a vast hydro-electric dam with the potential for creating great power. The waters were very full and deep behind the dam, but the water coming from the dam was only a very small steady trickle. The Christians were regulating the valves that would open and release the flow of the water. The more they were open to all that the Lord wanted to do, the more the power and flood of the Spirit would result.

There is no prayer that sums up the response we should make to the person of the Holy Spirit than one that thousands of Christians are using around the world today:

'Almighty God, we thank you for feeding us with the body and blood of your Son Jesus Christ. Through him we offer you our souls and bodies to be a living sacrifice. Send us out in the power of your Spirit to live and work to your praise and glory.'[6]

What Jesus did among that small band of committed believers, he has been doing constantly around the world. As men and women open their lives to his lordship, so they will open their lives to the power of his Spirit.


## For personal reflection or group study

1  The Holy Spirit often appears to bring division, although he is the Spirit of unity (Eph 4:3). Why do you think this is so?
2  In what ways do you chiefly need to know the power of the Spirit in your personal and church life?
3  What, in your experience, hinders Christians most from knowing the power of the Holy Spirit today? Are there practical steps you can take to solve this difficulty?

# 9   INCREASE OUR FAITH

'Where's daddy?'

'He's at a meeting.'

That is a familiar conversation in many a Christian home. In the last half of the twentieth century the church has been plagued with meetingitis – that is, meetings which inflame or irritate! Some Christian meetings inspire and excite us, others leave us feeling depressed. What makes the difference?

Lack of faith and vision is the major cause of this frustration. We need to adopt the disciples' request to Jesus: 'Increase our faith!' (Lk 17:5).

In this first part of the book, I have spelt out the principles upon which I believe we establish our corporate church life, and I have tried to explain what it will mean in practice to acknowledge the lordship of Jesus. None of these principles will operate unless we have faith. We need to walk by faith. I want, therefore, to answer four questions that are raised. What is faith?, Why is faith essential?, Where does faith begin? and How does faith grow?

## What is faith?

We need to be quite clear what we mean by 'faith', because the word itself is used in at least five different ways.

*There is 'the faith'* – 'I felt I had to write and urge you to contend for the faith that was once for all entrusted to the saints' (Jude 3). Jude is referring to the revealed truth of God that was taught by Christ and his apostles and written down in the scriptures. 'The faith' is the canon of what we believe. This cannot be increased.

*There is saving faith.* This is the faith that brings us into a right relationship with God through Jesus, once and for all. It is a relationship which we either have or do not have, so it cannot be increased. It is the faith of which both John and Paul have written: 'I tell you the truth, whoever hears my word and believes him who sent me has eternal life and will not be condemned; he has crossed over from death to life' (Jn 5:24) and 'Therefore, since we have been justified through faith, we have peace with God through our Lord Jesus Christ' (Rom 5:1).

*There is the gift of faith.* 'To one there is given through the Spirit the message of wisdom . . . to another faith by the same Spirit . . .' (1 Cor 12:8–9). Paul refers to this gift of faith again in 1 Corinthians 13:2 – it is the faith that moves mountains. Although Jesus in Mark 11:22–24 also speaks of faith that moves mountains, he is referring rather to the *quality* of faith that all Christians should seek to possess whereas the Corinthian passage refers to a *gift* that only some Christians have. Because it is a gift it cannot be increased; it can only be received and used.

*There is 'faithfulness' or 'perseverance'.* In Luke 18:8, as Jesus ends the parable of the widow and the unjust judge, our Lord poses the question: 'When the Son of Man comes, will he find faith on the earth?' Here Jesus implies our faithfulness.

Sometimes, as in 1 John 1:9 and 1 Thessalonians 5:24, such faithfulness is referring to the faithfulness of God. Where God's faithfulness is involved again it cannot be increased, because God is perfect.

*There is the faith that is the very heart of our relationship with and response towards God.* This is the faith that can be and needs to be increased. As Paul puts it: 'We live by faith, not by sight' or 'The life I live in the body, I live by faith in the Son of God, who loved me and gave himself for me' (2 Cor 5:7; Gal 2:20). The most familiar definition of faith – and indeed the only one in the whole of scripture – is in Hebrews 11: 'Now faith is being sure of what we hope for and certain of what we do not see . . . And without faith it is impossible to please God, because anyone who comes to him must believe that he exists and that he rewards those who earnestly seek him' (Heb 11:1,6).

I want to spend a little time getting this definition clearer. A number of writers help us to see what faith is *not*. William Barclay writes: 'It is not the hope that looks forward with wistful longing; it is the hope that looks forward with utter certainty. It is not the faith that takes refuge in a perhaps; it is the hope which is founded upon a conviction.'[1]

Another author writes, 'Faith is not positive thinking. Faith is not a hunch that is followed. Faith is not hoping for the best, hoping that everything will turn out alright. Faith is not a feeling of optimism. Faith is none of these things, though all of them have been identified as faith.'[2]

On the other hand, *faith is taking God at his word*.

'Faith', says the writer to the Hebrews, 'is the *substance* of things hoped for, the *evidence* of things not seen' (AV). The Greek word for 'substance' (*hupostasis*) literally means 'to stand under'. It is a foundation, a reality and a quality.[3] It is the same word used in Hebrews 1:3 to describe the very nature of Jesus. Faith is not just an idea or a concept. It has the very essence that gets things done. 'Evidence' really means proof or reproof. It can mean title-deeds, and the same word is used in 2 Timothy 3:16 about the scriptures that are profitable for teaching, for reproof, for correction.

So the faith that God looks for is to be as substantial and real as is the nature of Jesus himself, and it is as dynamic for action as is the very word of God. Faith is the key that unlocks doors; it is the hand of the beggar stretched out to take hold of what is being offered to it. 'Faith is not instinct, it is choice. The believer chooses to believe that God will keep his word. "Everything is possible for him who believes" (Mk 9:23)'.[4] Thus Charles Wesley could proclaim:

> Faith, mighty faith the promises sees
> And looks to God alone;
> Laughs at impossibilities,
> And cries, 'It shall be done!'[5]

Faith is the substance that drove William Carey on in his pioneer missionary work: 'Expect great things from God: attempt great things for God.' Faith was the hope that guided Martin Luther in his personal life and pastoral care of others.

The story is told of Luther meeting a peasant farmer who looked absolutely depressed. Luther asked him the cause of his gloom. The peasant replied that his house and stock had been destroyed by fire. He had lost everything and therefore life was not worth living. Martin Luther asked him if he knew the Apostles' Creed, and had the man recite it. 'I believe in God, the Father Almighty, maker of heaven and earth . . .' Luther had the farmer repeat those same words and then said that if he really believed the creed then there was absolutely no reason to be so gloomy. If God is the almighty Father then he could easily provide him with a new farm. Faith is taking God at his word.

## Why is faith essential?

Faith that takes God at his word and rests in trusting assurance, is the faith that works. Nowhere is this stated more clearly and fully than in Hebrews 11 – that great record of the heroes of faith. There we are told that it was by faith that Abel offered only the best to God; that Enoch reckoned walking with God was the most important concern in life; that Noah acted to save his whole household. It was by faith that Abraham obeyed God when in the eyes of the world it seemed stupid: he was willing to leave his security and live as a refugee in an uncertain world, and was able to obey God implicitly. It was by faith that Isaac could be concerned for the spiritual wellbeing of generations to come. It was by faith that Jacob and Joseph had confidence in the face of death. By faith Moses was willing to choose the way of suffering and hardship to lead God's people into the promised land, rather than enjoy the pleasures of the king's palace in Egypt. By faith that Joshua was able to lead the Israelites to the impossible victory over Jericho. And so the list continues, as indeed it does in Hebrews 11. They were all men and women who triumphed in life because they acted through faith.

When men and women have acknowledged the lordship of Jesus and followed him by faith, then things happen. A modern-day example would be that of the Sisters of Mary in Darmstadt in Western Germany.

As we lead visitors across our 'land of Canaan' today, what do they see? They see the Mother House and Chapel; the Jesus' Workshop, the large Jesus Proclamation Chapel, the retreat house for guests, Jesus' Joy; the small Francis convalescent home; twenty-two acres of land, plus all the grounds surrounding our buildings. They discover that we maintain a house in Israel. And how could all this have come about? Not through our merits, nor from great contributions or capital or mortgages. No. It came only out of great poverty, by means of faith and prayer. God proved that He stands by His word: *Give and it will be given to you . . . Seek ye first the kingdom of God . . . Whatever you ask in prayer, believe that you receive it, and you will.*[6]

This faith that works is often found in unlikely places, and unlikely people. For example, Jesus commended both the Roman centurion and the Canaanite woman for their faith that took God at his word and showed that faith works.

*The centurion (Lk 7:1–10).* He was a long-serving regular soldier in the Roman army with command of a hundred men. Here was a man who cared for his servant, loved the Jewish nation, had built the synagogue at Capernaum, and would protest that he was not worthy of the Lord's love and grace. Clearly he was not trusting in what he had achieved or deserved in any way. He was a Gentile and had no claim upon the mercy of Jesus. Yet he understood both Jesus' power and his authority. He realised that Jesus was Lord – subject to no one else except the Father – and that he was able to bring everything under his own control. He knew what obedience was, and that the spoken word was a creative word. Here was dynamic faith personally expressed: 'But say the word, and my servant will be healed.' Jesus declared his amazement at such faith, finding this beautiful trust in such an unexpected person, and went on to warn those who should have shown a similar faith of the danger they were in, before assuring the soldier that his faith had borne fruit. As Matthew's account says, Jesus told him: 'Go! It will be done just as you believed it would.' It concludes: 'And his servant was healed at that very hour.'

*The Canaanite woman (Mt 15:21–28)*. While the centurion had faith which took Jesus at his word, this woman had the faith that persevered and prayed through until the answer and blessing came.

Consider the barriers this mother faced as she brought the desperate needs of her demon-possessed daughter to Jesus: he was leaving the area – like catching someone you want to see just when they are going out of the front door; she knew she had no right to come and ask for God's help; Jesus did not give her any encouragement by his silence; and the disciples told her she was a positive nuisance and it would be better if she went away and coped with the enormous problem of her daughter by herself.

Yet faith gave her boldness to keep going. She knew Jesus was the only one who could help her. She had heard what he had done for others and she was beginning to understand something of who he was. Probably the inherent determination of a desperate mother also drove her on.

Through the healing of her daughter, she personally discovered the love and faith of the Lord Jesus for her, she learnt that God does hear and answer prayer, and Jesus himself commended her for her faith.

Would that there were more of this kind of faith in our churches and fellowships today! But what so often happens? We have already noted how the reactions of the disciples, faced with the need to feed the five thousand people who had listened to Jesus' teaching (Jn 6), reflect the way many of us would act. So does their reaction in this case. Often in the western world we look at the daunting situations we face and pull back because we don't have the resources to match the need. We survey the spiritual and material needs of the growing number of vast cities in today's world and we sense that the task of meeting those needs is impossible. We wrestle with the needs of our urban society and our inner city areas where once there was a fine Christian witness, but now where old churches have been sold for bingo halls or turned into worship centres for those of other faiths. Can the gospel take root again in such unattractive circumstances? Do we conclude – like Philip, when he was faced with the five thousand – that the situation is impossible?

The Lord Jesus is both the example and object of faith: he looked to the Father through the eyes of faith. He needed to exercise faith throughout his life and ministry. For him, faith was indispensable and unshakeable. Clearly it demanded active faith in God to feed five thousand people with five small loaves and two small fish! It required faith to raise Lazarus from the dead, to calm the storms on the Sea of Galilee, to restore sight to the blind, and to straighten the bent back of the widow, to cast demons out of Legion and, above all, to face the pain and agony of his cruel death upon a Roman cross.

We tend to assume that it was easy for Jesus – simply because he was Jesus. Our Lord had faith, and that faith was in his Father. John's gospel records over one hundred occasions when Jesus used the word 'Father'. When Jesus spoke about God to his disciples, he referred to 'the Father'; when he spoke about his own intimate personal relationship, he would say, 'My Father'; when he was expressing his faith in prayer he just cried, 'Father'. That was the secret of faith: he was willing to obey and to trust his heavenly Father – and we are called to enjoy that same trusting relationship as children of our heavenly Father.

In all these examples, from the ministry of Jesus, the men and women of the Old and New Testament, as well as

Christians down the years, we see that faith is essential because it is faith that works.

## Where does faith begin?

Faith comes as we grow in our understanding of God himself and his promises. Apart from Jesus himself, there is no more outstanding example of faith than that of Abraham.

While the actual story is recorded for us in Genesis 12–25, there are summaries in Hebrews 11 and Romans 4, where Paul writes:

> Against all hope, Abraham in hope believed and so became the father of many nations . . . Without weakening in his faith . . . he did not waver through unbelief regarding the promise of God, but was strengthened in his faith and gave glory to God, being fully persuaded that God had power to do what he had promised.
>
> (Rom 4:18–21)

As Abraham stepped out in faith, so he discovered more and more about the God in whom he trusted. He began by calling on the name of the Lord, without fully knowing the complete nature of his God (Gen 12:7–8). Then God revealed himself as the one who would protect him – 'I am your shield' (Gen 15:1). Then the Lord showed that he was the one who would plan for him – 'I am the Lord who brought you up' (Gen 15:7). Then Abraham was shown that God is El Shaddai (Gen 17:1). Finally, when Abraham was called to offer up his son Isaac and he found the ram caught by the horns in the bushes, he proclaimed: 'The Lord Will Provide – Jehovah Jireh' (Gen 22:14).

Our faith is to be in the name of the Lord, for the name of God describes the character of God. In the Old Testament there are many names for the Lord that speak of his power, his protection, his provision, his healing, his holiness, his nature as our shepherd and so on.[7]

One of the most inspiring modern-day missionary testimonies is that of the Overseas Missionary Fellowship, with over 950 workers from various Christian denominations serving the church in East Asia. The work was founded by Hudson Taylor in 1865 and from the beginning he ran the work on the principle that God would unfailingly meet all the needs of those he called to work for him. Today the twin 'banners' under which the work has been supported still remain: 'Hitherto has the Lord helped us' and 'Jehovah-Jireh, the Lord will provide.'

Hudson Taylor himself stated this principle of faith in this way:

> I do want you to realise this principle of working with God, and of asking Him for everything . . . Our Father is very experienced: he knows very well that his children wake up with a good appetite every morning, and he always provides breakfast for them: and he does not send his children supperless to bed . . . Depend upon it, God's work done in God's ways will never lack God's supplies.[8]

This quality of faith that the Lord longs to see active within our churches has at least four marks.

*It will be divinely based.* Faith is a response to the teaching, promises and call of God. It will be based upon the word of God the Father, it will be strengthened by the saving work of Jesus upon the cross and it will be witnessed to within our own hearts by the Holy Spirit.

Smith Wigglesworth was a Bradford plumber called by God to preach throughout the world. He was a man of faith who took God at his word. He was a man constantly reading and feeding upon the word of God. He believed that libraries made swollen heads, but the word of God made enlarged hearts, for faith comes by hearing and hearing comes by the word of God. Thus he counselled people everywhere to 'fill your head and your heart with the Scriptures. As you do so, you are sowing in your heart the seeds which the Spirit of God can germinate. You must be soaked and filled with the Word of God.'[9]

*It will have dynamic power.* As we have seen, faith is the key that releases God's gifts and power. George Müller was one of God's giants of faith. It did not matter whether he was concerned about the provision of food for the children under his care in Bristol, or the need to cross the Atlantic and arrive in Quebec on time for a meeting although fog had already delayed his boat. George Müller knew that faith in God changed situations.

Despite the unbelief and protests of the captain of the steamer in which he was travelling to Canada, George Müller knew the only way he would get through to Quebec in time was by prayer. It is recorded that Müller knelt down and prayed one of the most simple prayers. 'Captain, he said, I have known my Lord for fifty-seven years and there has never been a single day that I have failed to get an audience with the King. Get up, Captain and open the door and you will find the fog has gone.' The captain could only testify that the fog indeed had gone and that Müller was in Quebec on Saturday for his meeting.

Many of us in such a situation would need to confess our unbelief and scepticism. We need to turn in repentance to the Lord if the power of a dynamic faith is to be released again within our churches.

*It will be attacked by Satan.* But we have been commanded to take the shield of faith with which we can quench all the fiery darts of the evil one. A former generation would have been more familiar with the idea of arrows suddenly hurled at the Christian – a more relevant picture today would be the spiritual petrol bombs and terrorist attacks that Satan launches without warning at churches and believers. But we have been given the shield of faith.

The Roman shield was like the modern-day police riot shield; it protected the whole of a person and could be linked with other shields, unlike the dustbin lid that a passer-by might grab hold of to protect himself. Paul says that above all we are to take the shield of faith. That 'above all' has three aspects:

(a) We must use the shield of faith together with the other armour. It is of little use having the breastplate of righteousness and the helmet of salvation if we are not going to release active faith as well.
(b) It is the vital piece of armour, and
(c) We must take the shield in every situation. We must never leave it behind.

*It is capable of growth.* This quality of faith, based on the word and promises of God is what the disciples asked Jesus to increase. How, therefore, does faith grow?

## How does faith grow?

*Believe that faith is something that can grow.* Too many Christians settle for the kind of faith they had when they first believed in the Lord. But the Bible presents faith as a grain of mustard seed which though very small can become something very big (Lk 17:5-6; Mt 17:20-21). In the New Testament, people are described as having varying qualities of faith, some have no faith (Mk 4:40), little faith (Mt 6:30), are weak in faith (Rom 14:1), are strong in faith (1 Cor 16:13), or have great faith (Mt 8:10). Once we realise that faith can grow and become dynamic we shall begin to do something about it.

*Confess and repent of unbelief.* 'I do believe; help me overcome my unbelief!' (Mk 9:24), was not only the prayer of the father who brought his son to the disciples without success, it is the cry of most believers! Unbelief is the failure to trust our heavenly Father. It is the confession that our understanding of God is small.

There may be a refusal or unwillingness to believe on our part. We might be relying upon our own resources and understanding, so confession will need to be linked with repentance, but that in turn can lead on to praise and

worship of God. There may be deep and hidden barriers to
the release of faith – past failure, hurts and disobedience.
There may be wrong attitudes of resentment and bitterness. We need to allow the Lord to deal with all these – to
cleanse and remove them, so that once more we know his
power released by our faith.

*Strengthen your faith with the reading of God's word.* Faith
comes by hearing and hearing comes through the word of
God (Rom 10:17). The word of God is given to us in order
that we might become strong. It is like milk and meat to
feed our souls. But the word has to be read and a response
has to be made to it. The word, when read, will lead on to
active praise. Paul Billheimer has written: 'The element
that energises faith is praise. Perpetual, purposeful and
aggressive praise. Praise is the highest form of prayer
because it combines petition with faith.'[10]

*Express your faith in obedient action.* Such action may be
defensive action towards Satan, as we take the shield of
faith to parry the fiery darts he tries to throw at us. It should
also be responsive, taking the next practical step that Jesus
as Lord is calling us to in our personal discipleship.

Sometimes we are called to act in faith on our own, but
generally the church is called to respond as his body. Each
strand of faith is drawn together with others to produce a
strong band of faith. We help, encourage and support one
another in the walk and life of faith. Of course it is not
always so. When the twelve spies went to reconnoitre the
promised land (Num 13) they saw the good and fruitful land
but they also saw the giants who dwelt there. Ten brought
back the report that it was too difficult to conquer. They
failed to enter because of unbelief. But Caleb and Joshua
presented a minority report. They responded by faith to the
call and challenge of the Lord, and they were the only two
who were able to enter into the promised land and share in
its blessings. This is the spiritual element missing in many,
many churches and fellowships today. Too many churches
ask, 'What are we able to do?', 'What resources do we

possess?', rather than asking: 'What is the Lord calling us to do?'

The Lord is calling his church in every place to move forward in establishing the kingdom of God. The precise details of that move forward will differ widely. For some it will mean a real step of faith in relationship to evangelism; for others it will mean a new pattern of local leadership; for a third group it will relate to finance; for others it will relate to relationships with neighbouring churches – Protestant and Catholic. There are other things it could mean for individual believers: the challenge of the full-time ordained ministry or of work with the church in another part of the world; taking early retirement to be free for the service of the Lord; accepting an invitation to speak for the first time in public; being involved in a responsible position within the community as a Christian.

The list is almost endless, but the Lord will make clear by his Spirit what he is challenging us to do by faith.

## For personal reflection or group study

1 An increase in faith often begins with confession and repentance of unbelief. Intellectually we believe that God *can do* everything, but what do you believe God *will* do in your own church situation? Do you need to confess and repent of unbelief?

2 Read Matthew 14:22–36 and discover the various stages of fear and faith that Peter passed through in this memorable event. What does it teach you?

3 It has been said that 'the mountains of difficulty are the foothills of faith'. Hudson Taylor believed that God's work had three stages: impossible, difficult and done. What mountains and impossible situations do you face, and how is God using them to increase your faith?

# PART TWO

# 10 'MY LORD AND MY GOD'

It was a postcard with a picture of 'Garfield' on the front, teeth grinning and asking, 'Miss me?' It was written to our family by one of our younger church members, a lovely Christian girl, as she went to join one of the British Youth with a Mission (YWAM) Discipleship training courses for three months. 'Nine girls in my room and I'm on the bottom bunk . . . Only a few English people here . . . from all over the world – Africa, America, Europe, Australia and New Zealand. Come down and see me, we can have dinner.'

That postcard illustrated what God is doing in individual lives around the world. He is calling people of all ages to be his disciples.

It is David Watson who has written most fully on this theme of discipleship. He maintains that the Christian church has largely neglected the thrust of the great commission: to make disciples:

> The vast majority of western Christians are church-members, pew-fillers, hymn-singers, sermon-tasters, Bible-readers, even born-again-believers or Spirit-filled-charismatics – but not true disciples of Jesus. If we were willing to learn the meaning of real discipleship and actually to become disciples, the church in the West would be transformed, and the resultant impact on society would be staggering.[1]

At the heart of discipleship is a true understanding of what it means for Jesus to be Lord. Jesus is to be Lord not only of our corporate church life but of the individual member as well. Jesus called individual followers to him and challenged them to personal commitment to himself before he drew them together as his church. It was Peter who was challenged about his commitment before his death, and Thomas who was faced with the risen Christ and fell before him acknowledging him as, 'My Lord and my God!'

It is perfectly possible to think we are being an effective church member by our regular attendance, faithful giving, active service and patient witness, but it does not necessarily follow that we are a disciple of Jesus. It is not possible, however, to be a disciple of Jesus without also being a fully committed member of his body. Church membership and personal discipleship are linked together.

In the remaining few chapters, we shall attempt to work out what the lordship of Jesus means in a number of practical and personal areas of discipleship.

## What is discipleship?

The word 'disciple' is used in the New Testament in various ways:[2] it can refer to an adherent (Jn 6:66), a secret disciple (Jn 19:38), the twelve apostles (Mt 10:1), those who demonstrated their discipleship by abiding in his word (Jn 8:31), those who showed his love (Jn 13:35), those who bore fruit (Jn 15:8). It can relate to those who believed in him and openly confessed him. But essentially a disciple is a *learner* or a *follower* of a person. Discipleship is primarily a relationship to and a response to a master and involves activity and achievement.

*Fellowship with Christ.* A disciple is someone who knows Jesus. Discipleship implies not only head knowledge and knowing about Jesus, but also a personal experiential knowledge of Jesus.

The Greek language has different words to mean 'begin to know' (*ginosko*) and 'to go on growing in your knowledge to complete and mature understanding' (*epignosko*). Thus Paul saw his aim as not just having people receive Jesus Christ as Lord (Col 2:6–7), but as presenting them mature in Christ (Col 1:28–29). Discipleship is an ongoing relationship. Discipleship is not a part-time occupation, it is a total and lifelong commitment of ourselves to the Lord. It is not a matter of trying to be a Christian on a Sunday: it requires that we follow the Lord as his disciples Monday to Saturday as well, working out our discipleship at home and school, in the office and factory, in illness and on holiday.

*Friendship with Jesus.* Discipleship includes not only knowing Jesus, but loving him. The Christian life is a marvellous love affair with the Son of God. As Jesus said to his inner team, 'I have called you friends' (Jn 15:13–15). A friend is much more than a companion. A friend is someone who is greatly loved and very dear to us.

I have in my possession a letter my wife and I treasure. It is from a lady called Penny. She had been finding life very tough although she had been a Christian for many years. There had been pressures on her marriage and home life, ending in divorce. The children were growing up and she had been through a long period of rejection, bitterness, resentment, self-pity and was not at all sure that God loved her. She ends her letter as follows: 'He reached down from on high and took hold of me; He drew me out of deep waters. He rescued me from my powerful enemy . . . the Lord was my support. He brought me out into a spacious place, He rescued me BECAUSE HE DELIGHTED IN ME.'

When we know the love and friendship of Jesus like that it will radically change every area of our lives. It will affect our mind and thinking, our emotions and affections. It will influence the holidays we book, the car we buy, the possessions we value, the moral comments we make. The lordship of Jesus covers everything, and if he is not Lord of all, then he is not Lord at all.

*Listening to and following Jesus.* We have already considered what it means for the church to listen corporately to the Lord as its head, and allow him to direct the action of the body (see chapter three). In many ways it will mean the same thing for every disciple. We are called to listen to his

voice and follow in his footsteps. Jesus never varied that
command. It was the same invitation – 'Follow me' – that he
gave to the disciples when he first called them, when he
commissioned them, and when he re-called them. Often
Jesus meets the attitude, 'Lord I will follow you, but let me
first go and . . .' That is a clear contradiction in terms. How
can he be Lord if we dictate the terms on which we follow as
his disciples?

Peter had been called to follow Jesus, he had made a
miserable failure of his first efforts and could so easily have
given up, but Jesus set him free from his foolish failure, his
early enthusiasms, his stubborn self-will, his curiosity and
concern about John's ability to follow the Lord, and his
headstrong and isolated individualism.

Peter and Andrew were called to leave their nets, their
fishing and their father in order to follow Jesus. Likewise a
man is called to leave his father and mother before he can
truly cleave to his wife and become one flesh. Even so, the
disciple must leave the things that are not of Christ if he
would cleave closely to his Lord and follow him wherever
he leads.

We cannot serve two masters. We will either hate the one
and love the other or we will be devoted to the one and
despise the other. We cannot serve both God and money
(Mt 6:24).

Essentially then, discipleship involves increasingly
knowing Jesus, unashamedly loving him and obediently
following him throughout our lives.

## Jesus is Lord

Jesus calls us to discipleship simply because he is Lord. The
title Lord, or *kurios*, was used by believers only to address
God or Jesus. It was the New Testament Greek equivalent
of the Hebrew word 'Jehovah' in the Old Testament.
Jehovah is used more than 6,800 times as a title for God and
also for Christ. 'He is the ever-living One, the only-living
One, the self-existent One, and is dependent on no one or

nothing outside Himself. He is self-existent and self-sufficient.'[3]

Jesus was declared to be Lord as a result of his resurrection from the dead: 'Therefore let all Israel be assured of this: God has made this Jesus, whom you crucified, both Lord and Christ', '[He] was declared with power to be the Son of God, by his resurrection from the dead: Jesus Christ our Lord' (Acts 2:36; Rom 1:4).

As Lord he has rights and authority over us. A barrister friend has pointed out to me that we use the word 'rights' in a number of ways, all of which illuminate our understanding of the right or lordship of Jesus.

First, 'rights' give one person a claim against another. If, for example, a stranger was obstructing the access to my front door, I would have the right to insist that he made way and allowed me the right of entry into my own property. In the same way, Jesus has a right to insist that he is allowed into the lives that he has made and redeemed, and he will resist the counter-claims of Satan, who stands and bars the way.

Second, 'rights' can imply privilege. Diplomatic privilege is given to staff and officials of a foreign country's delegation in another country. Their baggage is not searched at airports and their officers cannot be searched by the police. It is their right and privilege. Likewise Jesus is free from the claims that Satan might try to make against him, and in so far as we are 'in Christ', we too share that same right and privilege.

Thirdly, 'rights' imply power. Through my position as a minister of the Church of England I have the power to pronounce a couple man and wife together, and to alter irrevocably their relationship to each other, to their families and to society. Likewise, Jesus through his office as saviour and risen Lord has the power to alter the relationship between sinful man and a holy God.

Thus *kurios* is not only a title, it suggests a position of authority of one person over another. It was that position which Thomas recognised when he confessed Jesus as Lord and God. It was that position which Jesus claimed when the disciples acknowledged that all authority and power had been given to him and they were to go and make disciples in his name.

## Working it out in daily life

Christian discipleship is both corporate, radical and personal. Some local churches have expressed the link between church membership and personal discipleship in a statement which they ask all intending church members to accept. For example, a Baptist church in the North of England expressed the out-working of discipleship in these terms:

> At the heart of our fellowship's life is a desire and determination to live under the lordship (the kingly, authoritative, decisive rule) of Jesus Christ, both in our individual and corporate walk with him. Jesus wants disciples, and he has the right to disciple us, if we are his, in every area of our lives – our home, family, money, work, plans, hopes and even our church! We are resolved to walk the path of radical discipleship with Jesus, believing that anything less is a denial of his lordship. This means a readiness to change anything within our lives, or within our church that he points out to us.[4]

While some Christians will see discipleship in corporate terms, others will understand it in very radical terms.

Jim Wallis, for example, had been brought up in America in a conventional Christian home. As he faced the social order in America and the tensions of the black ghettos confronted by the white American police, as he faced the call to join in the Vietnam war, as he experienced the peaceful protest movement of the American universities of the 1960s, he was seeking to work out in personal and daily terms what it meant to be a disciple of the Lord Jesus. It was through hearing again the radical and revolutionary teaching and demands of the sermon on the mount that Jim Wallis came to commit his life to Jesus: 'The Sermon on the Mount revealed to me what Jesus meant by the Kingdom of God. In it, Jesus calls those who would follow him to a life that completely undermines the values and structures of this world and opens up the possibilities of a new one.'[5] Again: 'I finally knew that I wanted to be a follower of this Jesus. Contrary to the message I had received from the Church, Jesus' message was as political as it was personal, as economic as it was spiritual, having as much to do with public life as individual devotion.'[6]

But what will discipleship mean for most Christians in their local churches and fellowship? Just as the essence of Christian marriage is found not in a long list of activities to be fulfilled but in a simple attitude of love and submission to be worked out day by day, so the heart of Christian discipleship consists not in feverish action but in following Jesus, denying ourselves and taking up the cross.

As Jesus put it: 'If anyone would come after me, he must deny himself and take up his cross and follow me. For whoever wants to save his life will lose it, but whoever loses his life for me will find it' (Mt 16:24–25; see also Mt 10:32–39). The wisdom of these conditions is reflected in Jim Elliot's words: 'He is no fool who gives what he cannot keep to gain what he cannot lose.' What was it, then, that Jesus was asking of his disciples?

*We must deny ourselves.* Jesus was not talking about giving things up for Lent, or putting £5 in a self-denial envelope once in a while. He wasn't asking us to yield him time, or money, but rather yield ourselves to him. We need to dethrone ourselves and place Christ firmly and for ever upon the throne of our lives. It means that we move over from the driving seat of the car of our lives, and are willing to remain in the passenger seat – or even the back seat – and trust Christ with the driving, the destination and the direction that we take to get there. We hand over control and that is one of the most difficult things for most of us.

Jesus taught the same lesson in this way:

I tell you the truth, unless a grain of wheat falls to the ground and dies, it remains only a single seed. But if it dies, it produces many seeds. The man who loves his life will lose it, while the man who hates his life in this world will keep it for eternal life.

(Jn 12:24–25)

The only way to live for Christ is to die.

*We must take up the cross.* In a century which has witnessed more martyrs for Christ than any other, taking up the cross may literally mean death. It will very certainly mean that we die to self, ambition and this world. As Bishop J. C. Ryle comments: 'True Christianity brings with it a daily cross in this life. The flesh must be daily crucified, the devil must daily be resisted and the world must be daily overcome.'[7]

A young man once asked an older Christian, 'What does it mean to be crucified with Christ?' The older man thought for a moment, and then replied: 'To be crucified with Christ means three things. First, the man who is crucified is facing only one direction; he is not looking back. Second, the man who is crucified has said goodbye to the world; he is not going back. Third, the man who is crucified has no further plans of his own. He is totally in God's hands. Whatever the situation, he says, "Yes, Lord!"'[8]

A successful dentist was faced with the challenge of God's call to the Christian ministry. God showed him his life and it was full of light, with the exception of one dark area. That darkness was the status he was hanging on to. Having battled in that area, he wisely and humbly yielded to Jesus. It will be different for others. It may be dying to security in anything other than Jesus. It may be dying to comfort and the refusal to move from a pleasant area and away from friends. It may be dying to an unwillingness to face new challenges or dying to God-given and natural instincts. One thing is sure, however: when we die, we shall live. When we offer up precious things to Jesus, he gives us back more than ever we gave to him.

*We must follow Jesus.* Jesus has claimed the right to our loyalty and allegiance: we shall be identified with him. When we commit ourselves to Jesus, we automatically change every other relationship in our lives.

Dr John White is an eminent psychiatrist and Christian writer. In *The Cost of Commitment* he shares an early experience as a medical student:

> I had missed one of the clinical sessions at a treatment center for venereal diseases. To make up for lost time I was obliged to go to the clinic at night, when medical students did not normally attend. As I entered the door, a strong male nurse took me by the arm and pushed me into a line of shabbily dressed men awaiting treatment.
>
> 'Excuse me, I've come to see the doctor in charge,' I tried to explain.
>
> 'So have all the rest,' the nurse replied. 'Wait your turn.'
>
> 'You don't understand, I'm a medical student.'
>
> 'That's all right, sonny, medical students get it the same way as everyone else.'
>
> Eventually I got him to understand that I was part of the treatment team, not a patient. But I had learned something. I had learned how huge was the chasm between 'us' and 'them' and how unwilling I was to cross that chasm and identify myself with patients suffering from V.D. I have since then been filled with wonder at the chasm Jesus (who knew no sin) crossed to stand beside us sinners, waiting to be baptized.[9]

Jesus was not ashamed of us, and he asks that we are not ashamed of him in our discipleship. We are not to be ashamed of his name. Though some are embarrassed to mention 'Jesus' in public, we are not to be ashamed of his church and friends – even though some of us do 'disown' other Christians if they are in any way 'odd'. We are not to be ashamed of his message and his salvation, and we are not to be ashamed of the commitment we have made to him.

Jesus not only stated clearly the demands that he called for, but he set out the reasons for them. Jesus knew that the things which really matter are spiritual and eternal, not physical and passing: 'What good will it be for a man if he gains the whole world, yet forfeits his soul? (Mt 16:26). He knew that personal fulfilment, effective Christian living and victory come when we face the demands of discipleship and put him first. It is Luke who records that Jesus has a sovereign right to make these demands of discipleship upon us because he had first of all faced them for us (Lk 14:25–35).

It has been said that the entrance fee into the Christian life is nothing, but the annual subscription is everything. I need to receive him into my life as Lord, and to confess openly with my lips that I have yielded my allegiance to him.

The believers at Colosse received Christ Jesus as Lord because one of them, Epaphras, came back from hearing Paul preach the gospel somewhere else, and himself began to share with his friends back home in Colosse the truth of God's grace in Jesus towards sinners. When they heard and understood the good news, having learnt it from Epaphras, they responded to the message with faith, and received Christ into their hearts (Col 1:3–8; 2:6–7).


## The blessing of discipleship

We sometimes forget that the master has responsibilities towards his disciples. We not only commit ourselves to him, he commits himself to each one of us.

We have been given the power and authority of the master's name as we seek to serve him (Acts 2:21; 3:16; 8:16). In return he has promised us his protection and provision. If we first seek his kingdom, then our heavenly Father, who knows what we need, will give us the basic things of life as well (Mt 6:33). Or as Samuel stated in the Old Testament, the Lord has said, 'Those who honour me I will honour' (1 Sam 2:30).

From time to time we have the joy of taking teams from our church to other churches for ministry. One weekend, four of us were away on a house party, and I asked each of the other three to testify to the lordship of Jesus in their lives. One testified to receiving the fullness of his Spirit as she yielded to his lordship. One, a young wife, told of the time before she was married when she longed to be married. She had a demanding job as a teacher and wanted a change, had been asked to lead a Christian camp for girls, and finally had discovered a lump in her breast! On each occasion she faced the challenge to make Jesus Lord. As she yielded and honoured him, so Jesus dealt with every situation. The lump was found to be benign, she was given strength to lead the camp, given a different class to teach, and then met the man she would later marry! The third person to testify was her husband, a man gaining rapid promotion in his work and often having to travel with his colleagues overseas, thus facing all the temptations of the world – money, sex and big business. He knew that he had to make it quite clear early on, firmly but graciously, that Jesus was his master and that completely different values and attitudes governed his life. Instead of spending a Sunday in Brazil indulging the flesh, he was to be found with a group of fellow believers worshipping the Lord.

A young law student who came to England in the 1970s from Hong Kong also testifies to finding a faith in Jesus while in England, and then God's provision as he sought to honour him in every way: 'Through a totally unexpected channel and in a most miraculous way, God has graciously provided me with over £30,000 in the four years when I did my law degree and read for Bar Finals in London. Not only has the Lord looked after me like a Father looks after his children materially, but also he has enabled me to finish my studies by constantly giving me strength, courage and wisdom.'

Jesus made it clear that the blessing and rewards he

promises his disciples relate not only to this world but also to the world to come: 'Everyone who has left houses or brothers or sisters or father or mother or children or fields for my sake will receive a hundred times as much and will inherit eternal life. But many who are first will be last, and many who are last will be first' (Mt 19:29–30).

## The response of the disciple

There is, thus, only one response worthy of the disciple: obedience to our Lord and master. That was the reaction of the Son to the Father, and it is to be the response of the disciple to his master.

It is said that Jesus learnt obedience. He came to understand and experience the meaning and reality of obedience through his suffering. Yet he trusted his heavenly Father so fully that he was able to obey him completely.

If we would reflect the character of our master, fulfil the commission of our Lord, experience the blessing of our king, and fulfil the purpose and calling of our personal discipleship, then we shall seek to obey the Son. Such obedience will not be the condition of being his disciple, but it will be the evidence that we are.

## For personal reflection or group study

1 Is there a difference between 'being a Christian' and 'being a disciple'?
2 Look up Luke 14:25–35. What do you think the three conditions

   o 'If anyone . . .' (v.26)
   o 'anyone who does not . . .' (v.27)
   o 'any of you who do not . . .' (v.33)

mean in today's world?
3 How can Christians be positively and attractively different from other people, without being seen as dull and negative by non-Christians?

# 11  TOTAL MAN

There are more Jewish people living in London than in Jerusalem, and there are larger Jewish communities in America than in the whole of Israel.[1] We live in the London borough which has the greatest concentration of Jewish people, and it was not surprising for our children to be invited to the Bar Mitzvah of their friends. The Bar Mitzvah is a great family occasion combining a religious service and a family feast. At the age of thirteen a Jewish boy becomes a 'Son of the law'.

'The law' has a central place in the life and thinking of the Jews (see Exod 21–23; Lev 17–26; Deut 12–26). Thus, when the Pharisees, the experts in the Jewish law, gathered together to discuss the question to ask Jesus, they asked: 'Teacher, which is the greatest commandment in the Law?'

> Jesus replied, '"Love the Lord your God with all your heart and with all your soul and with all your mind." This is the first and greatest commandment. And the second is like it: "Love your neighbour as yourself." All the Law and the Prophets hang on these two commandments.'
>
> (Mt 22:37–40)

Jesus had linked together the law relating to God (Deut 6:5) and the law relating to people (Lev 19:18) and pronounced that these two statements included within them the total law and commandment of God to people.

In giving the Pharisees the perfect answer, Jesus also gave us a marvellous summary of what his lordship means for men and women. Jesus asks that all of us responds in love and obedience to all of him: we are to acknowledge his lordship with our heart, soul and mind – and other versions add 'strength'.

'Total man' is to respond to the lordship of Jesus. In this

chapter I want to focus on some neglected but vital areas of Christ's lordship – he is Lord of our minds, of our emotions and reactions, and of our bodies.

## Lord of our minds

'The mind denotes the seat of reflective consciousness, comprising the faculties of perception and understanding and those of feeling, judging and determining.'[2] Put more simply, just as the steering on a car determines where the car goes, so our minds direct what our bodies do. Like every other part of us, however, our minds have been affected by sin, but they can be transformed by God's love and grace. Consider the following, for example: 'Those who live according to the sinful nature have their minds set on what that nature desires; but those who live in accordance with the Spirit have their minds set on what the Spirit desires' (Rom 8:5; see also Eph 4:17–24; 1 Cor 2:16).

Our minds are not neutral territory. They are a frequent battleground for the clash of the kingdoms. They are controlled either by sin and self, or they are submitted to the saviour, to his Spirit and to the Word of God. How we use our minds will govern our daily living. Consider Paul's letter to the Philippians, where he refers at least four times to our minds.

*Purity of mind.* 'Finally, brothers, whatever is true, whatever is noble, whatever is right, whatever is pure, whatever is lovely, whatever is admirable – if anything is excellent or praiseworthy – think about such things' (Phil 4:8). How easy it is to allow thoughts of bitterness or resentment about a person, the conditions in which we live and work, the way we were treated by someone else, and a hundred and one other reactions to influence our life. We shall find that this relates to the papers we read, the books and magazines we pick up, the TV and video programmes we watch, the conversations we have – or overhear – and the control of our minds. According to Paul, our minds should be like a fortress guarded against assault, with Jesus in control and our thoughts kept in check and not allowed to break out and run just where they want to (2 Cor 10:5).

*Humility of mind.* 'Each of you should look not only to your own interests, but also to the interests of others. Your attitude should be the same as that of Christ Jesus . . .' (Phil 2:4–5). Presumption, arrogance and all the self-words – self-centred, self-interest, etc. – are the opposites of humility of mind. Pride is the opposite of loving the Lord with all our heart and mind. Humility of mind will help us to have the right attitude towards the Lord, towards others and towards ourselves. Here again, we express in practical terms what it means to have Jesus as Lord.

*Single-mindedness.* Paul has been writing about his own desire to press on to fulfil the calling and purpose God has for his life. He continues: 'I press on towards the goal to win the prize for which God has called me heavenwards in Christ Jesus. All of us who are mature should take such a view of things' (Phil 3:14–15). Men are motivated by different philosophies – materialism, pleasure, success, ambition, political ends, comfort, etc. What they have set their minds on will determine what they achieve. Jesus sought always to do those things that would please the Father. He did not seek to please himself, but the Father who had sent him (see Jn 5:30; 8:29; Rom 15:1–3).

*Peace of mind.* 'The Lord is near. Do not be anxious about anything, but in everything, by prayer and petition, with thanksgiving, present your requests to God. And the peace of God, which transcends all understanding, will guard your hearts and your minds in Christ Jesus' (Phil 4:5–7). There are a hundred and one reasons why people are anxious today. The threat of a nuclear war, the increase of violence, the growing possibilities of unemployment, the breakdown of marriages and family life, the distress and ruin brought to countless lives through famine, drug and alcohol abuse, the anxiety of parents for their children, and the escalation of terrorism are only matched by the restlessness and concern of the human spirit inwardly. The scriptures show us that there is only one answer: – to acknowledge in practice the sovereignty and lordship of Jesus. Our minds are to be known for their purity, humility, purpose and peace. They are also to be active, not passive, minds.

It has been said, 'Many evangelical Christians are very well read in their profession and even in their hobbies but do not regard it as a responsibility to be well read in matters of the faith.'[3] And again: 'Fundamentally, to love God with all our mind is to let God's revealed truth work through our lives so that our thinking, our attitudes, our worship and our deeds are *consistent*.'[4]

While the Bible is a record of God's plan and purpose of salvation, not a blue-print with ready-made answers for life in a sophisticated technological space age, nevertheless there are revealed in it guidelines and principles that enable us to work out the Christian's response to many areas of life.

Today Christians are seeking to work out economic and political issues, the biblical attitude to homelessness and single-parent families, and a whole host of other questions which tax our minds. But this is only part of the outworking of what it means to love the Lord with all our mind.

In practice it means we shall give time to read widely on Christian issues, and we shall use our critical faculties in the reading of the Bible. Unafraid of the truth, we shall not allow ourselves to be people whose Christian lives are like blotting paper, unthinkingly soaking up all that is written and spoken without questioning it and examining it in the light of the scriptural revelation. We shall begin to think biblically.

The process may be painful and costly, and almost certainly Christians will not always agree with each other, but, as Jim Wallis discovered, once you decide to allow Jesus to be Lord of every part of life, he will challenge and change many aspects: 'The Word of God is intended to judge all our priorities, to overturn all our biases, to correct all our perceptions.'[5]

Applying the word of God to the issues of the day is a process to be worked at by all Christians.

Before they became Christians some people's minds may have been occupied with things that hurt and seared them, resulting in a need for a ministry of healing to the memories – but God is perfectly able to do that. We will have to deal with the fear that grips our mind. As a friend wrote to us: 'It was a sure and certain work of the Lord, and I have lost the fear that was previously like background music . . . I sense that with healing like this, affecting thought patterns and imagination, it is necessary for me to "work out" the healing by discipling my mind with scripture.'

We are rediscovering the ministry of healing in all its aspects. Healing is wholeness. 'The human being is an interrelated, interconnected and interdependent unity of body, soul (mind, memories and emotions) and spirit. What happens in one part will inevitably affect the other parts sooner or later.'[6] Our minds and our emotions, our spirit and our bodies are all interdependent. What we are thinking with our minds will be expressed in our speech, shown in our emotions and may well become visible in our bodies. As Donald Bridge has written:

> Physical ailments really are often caused by inward attitudes, mental conditions and emotional shocks. Stomach ulcers are (sometimes) caused by worry. Arthritis seemed to be (sometimes) linked with bitterness of spirit. Headaches can be caused by frustration, paralysis by guilt, asthma by fear. Depressed people are more open to infection. Anger releases a flow of harmful chemicals into the body. Hurt administered long ago poisons the subconscious memory and leads to illness.[7]

Surely it makes sense to model our emotional reactions upon the pattern of Jesus, and to allow him to be Lord of our inward spirit, not just because he is Lord, but because it is the way of wholeness and personal blessing.

## Lord of our emotions

'Emotions must always be accountable to the faculties of
reason and will . . . Satan is devastatingly effective in using
the weapons of guilt, rejection, fear, embarrassment, grief,
depression, loneliness and misunderstanding. Indeed
human beings are vulnerable creatures who could not
withstand these satanic pressures without divine assist-
ance.' How glad we can be to know that 'we do not need to
be victims of our emotions'.[8] We shall consider three
emotions that are common to us all – anger, guilt and love.

### Anger

We might readily assume that anger is automatically sinful,
but that is not always so. The Bible speaks of the anger of
God, and we read that Jesus himself was angry. He looked
around at the people in the synagogue who were more
concerned to obey the letter of the law about the sabbath
than to bring the grace of healing to the man with a
shrivelled hand, and he was angry.

There are many biblical references to the anger of God
(e.g. Num 11:1; Deut 29:27; Ps 103:8; 145:8). As Myra
Chave-Jones, former director of Care and Counsel has
written: 'It is all summed up in Ezra 8:22 "The power of his
anger is against all who forsake him" – in whatever way
they turn to other guidelines for life. God's anger is about
His eternal justice, His own righteousness and His love
which is beyond the comprehension of the human mind.'[9]
As R. G. V. Tasker has written, 'It is rather a personal
quality, without which God would cease to be fully righteous and his love would degenerate into sentimentality.'[10]

Thus it is quite plain that there are times when the
Christian – if Jesus is Lord of his or her life – should be
angry: *not* to be angry in such circumstances will be sinful.
Anger is energy that drives men and women to act against
all that denies the love and life and lordship of Jesus. There
will be various occasions in society and circumstances
in human lives – circumstances of unrighteousness,

exploitation, indifference, moral decline or rebellion – when the Christian should be moved by anger to act in the name of Christ.

But there are also times – as probably all of us know – when anger stems from other sources. As James Dobson points out, it can arise from extreme fatigue, embarrassment, frustration and rejection.[11] In such cases it is a cry for help.

How are Christians to handle such a powerful emotion as anger and allow Jesus to be Lord? Whether it is personal anger in the home or political anger in the nation, let me suggest the following guidelines:

*Recognise that anger is a justifiable emotion, but that it can be twisted and become sinful.* Hence Paul can counsel the Ephesians: 'In your anger do not sin: Do not let the sun go down while you are still angry' (Eph 4:26).

*Respond to the impulses of anger quickly, positively and specifically.* How easy it is for words such as 'You always . . .' or 'You never . . .' to be spoken in anger. Such remarks are usually unfair and untrue – but they have resulted from an anger that has been allowed to go on unchecked.

*Refuse to bring up the past.* Present anger will try to justify its actions by calling for evidence from the past. The defence will, in turn, call witnesses on its behalf against the one who is angry, and so an angry thought leads to angry words, and the process continues until the people recognise that a relationship has been broken. It will only be restored when there is the willingness to confess sin and to repent of the wrong attitudes and forgive.

*Be ready to examine the real problem.* In almost all cases anger is the symptom and not the cause of the trouble. Thus, instead of being destructive, anger can, if handled aright, become a constructive and positive force in our lives.

*Reaffirm your commitment to the person you are angry with.*
Whether it is anger in a marriage or anger amongst a group
of people, this is essential. Instead of the works of the flesh,
among which are all the family of anger – hatred, discord,
jealousy, fits of rage, selfish ambition, dissensions, factions
and envy – there can grow the whole family of love and joy
and peace, patience, kindness, goodness and self-control.
The fruit of the Spirit will grow where Jesus is allowed to be
Lord.

As John Henry Jowett once said, 'The will of God
will never lead you where the grace of God cannot keep
you.'[12]


## Guilt

Anger can easily lead to guilt. A person will feel guilty
about something they have or have not done. They will feel
guilty about the distant past or the immediate present. Why
is this, and how do we handle it, so that we demonstrate the
lordship of Jesus?

'Guilty' is the verdict that our conscience pronounces
upon our lives. It is the judge that assesses our actions and
thoughts.[13]

David is an outstanding example of someone who sup-
pressed his conscience and denied that he had sinned, until
Nathan, sent by God, announced to him, 'You are the
man!', at which point David broke down in confession, and
found a freedom from his guilt and a peace in his conscience
for the first time since he had sinned against Bathsheba and
Uriah (2 Sam 11–12). We dishonour Jesus as Lord of every
part of our lives so long as we refuse to acknowledge actual
and specific sin in our lives.

Christ is able to deal with all guilt, whether it is true guilt
or false guilt. True guilt is the result of the Holy Spirit
convicting us of sin. It is a clear signal from God that there is
something wrong in our lives that must be put right. We
recognise it, repent of it and experience his cleansing.
Satan, however, comes along as the accuser of the
brethren, and as the father of lies, seeking to turn the

situation into one of false guilt, and many Christians have to battle with this.

There are several causes of false guilt. It may arise from the unrealistic and unreasonable hopes and expectations of parents for their children.

How easy it is for our western society to place the wrong values on its attitudes to children, and indeed to adults as well. Take, for example, a beautiful child and a plain one: we can so easily give more importance to the beautiful child. Or consider an intellectually very bright child and one who cannot pass exams: we give the impression that the clever child is more valuable. Or imagine that we are in touch with a child from a very wealthy home and one from a poor home: we could so easily pay more attention to the child with money behind him. By our attitudes we are sending our own clear signals that we consider beauty, intelligence and wealth to be more important and valuable, and in so doing we can easily make the other child feel inferior and guilty. We need to recognise that this is a common failure and, instead of making others feel guilty, we should confess that we ourselves have been guilty.

We proclaim the lordship of Jesus as we reflect his values and as we recognise the distinction between true and false guilt – confessing the one and resisting the other.

## Love

Commenting on the beatitude 'Blessed are the pure in heart', Martyn Lloyd-Jones has defined the heart as the centre of our personality. 'The "heart" in Scripture . . . is the centre of man's being and personality; it is the fount out of which everything else comes. It includes the mind; it includes the will; it includes the heart. It is the total man . . .'[14]

There is no clearer reflection of the lordship of Jesus in our lives than through our love.

'My command is this: Love each other as I have loved you' (Jn 15:12). That command is to apply not only within the Christian fellowship but also within the Christian family. Husbands are to love (*agape*) their wives as Christ has loved us (Eph 5:25). We are so to experience the love of God in our own hearts that we are able to show that love to others.

What does this mean in daily living? Let me focus on two aspects:

*The motive for our love.* Paul makes the remarkable statement in Romans 5:5–10 that God's love is shown towards four categories of people: towards the helpless (v.6) – those who are incapable, unable and powerless to respond to God; towards the ungodly (v.6) – those who are out of harmony with God (the picture is that of members of an orchestra all playing out of tune with each other and out of time with the conductor); towards the sinner (v.8) – those who have fallen short and missed the mark of God's standards; and towards the enemy (v.10) – those who are hostile towards and opposed to God himself.

Making Christ Lord and loving as he loves means that we are willing and, through his provision, able to love the person in the office who constantly makes our lives utterly miserable. It means the wife is able to go on loving her husband who keeps her short of housekeeping and comes home the worse for drink and who has spent all his wages on gambling. Rightly, she will hate his sin or illness, but will seek to love him. It will mean that we can love those who steal from us while opposing the crime. It means loving the person who murders a member of our family, and such is happening in Northern Ireland.

*The manner of our love.* No description of love excels that given by Paul in 1 Corinthians 13. The particular context in which it comes is Paul's teaching about the use of spiritual gifts in the church, but its truth is applicable to every aspect of life.

Love is patient and kind; it is not jealous or conceited or proud; love is not ill-mannered or selfish or irritable; love does not keep a record of wrongs; love is not happy with

evil, but is happy with the truth. Love never gives up, and
its faith, hope, and patience never fail.

(1 Cor 13:4–7 GNB)

If you substitute the name of 'Christ' for love, the passage
still rings true. If, on the other hand, you change 'love' for
'I', then it sounds false and hollow. Thus we see very
quickly our *need* of love as well as the *nature* of love. We are
constantly having to work at this perfecting of love towards
others.


## Lord of our bodies

The lordship of Jesus is to rule over every aspect of our
being. We have considered in some detail his lordship of
our minds and of our emotions – especially our anger, guilt
and love. We have seen that his lordship is to affect the
value we assign to other people. Jesus' lordship is also to
rule over our physical bodies.

Perhaps there is no time in history when more attention is
paid to the human body. But what should be the attitude of
the Christian who has made Jesus Lord?

*We are to accept our bodies as part of God's creation and not
despise them.* Some people may consider themselves too
short or tall, fat or thin. Some have suffered damage at
birth or inherited big ears and feel that they are not
attractive. It is so easy to despise our bodies and to resent
what God has given to us. But the Bible tells us that God
has made our bodies and he knows what our bodies need
(Gen 1:26–31). He is concerned for the body as well as for
the soul (Heb 10:5), so that not even one hair of our head is
overlooked (Mt 6:25–34; 10:29–31).

*We are to recognise that sin has marred our bodies and
twisted our appetites.* All the human appetites are God-
given – the appetites for food, love, sex, action, etc. are
God-given and all these activities are God-ordained, but

sin has corrupted them, so that, for example, eating can be misused and the sexual appetites can be despised or misdirected (Rom 1:24). We need to beware of the dangers of misusing our bodies, but not to the extent that we end up not using them at all!

*Our bodies are indwelt by the Holy Spirit of Jesus.* As temples of God (1 Cor 6:13,19–20) our bodies need to be kept pure and clean, both physically and spiritually. We would not want to use our bodies in ways that would displease the Spirit of Jesus. The lordship of Jesus will affect our leisure habits, our recreation, the things that we eat and drink and the amount of sleep that we have. We are to keep our bodies in a fit state, so that our minds and spirits are as healthy as possible.

*Our bodies will be replaced.* Even when our bodies become old, feeble and wear out,[15] we know that they will be replaced with a marvellous resurrection body – similar to that which we have lived in, but different in that it won't be subject to time and space (1 Cor 15; 2 Cor 5:1–4; Phil 3:21). Our future spiritual bodies are not affected by what happens to our mortal bodies at the time of death. Through burial or cremation they will decay and be no more. But the Lord has promised to give to those who love him a new spiritual body when we go to be with him.

The Lord's attitude to the body is clearly shown by his incarnation. Jesus came in the flesh. He grew in wisdom and stature. He experienced tiredness and sadness, hunger and pain, rest and human companionship – all in the body.

As Paul reminds the Corinthians, 'Do you not know that your body is a temple of the Holy Spirit, who is in you, whom you have received from God? You are not your own; you were bought at a price. Therefore honour God with your body' (1 Cor 6:19–20). And, he might have continued, 'with your emotions, your mind and your whole being'!

# For personal reflection or group study

1 In what ways has this chapter helped you to understand more about the lordship of Jesus over you as a whole person?

2 Consider what it means, in practical terms, to set the mind on the things of the Spirit or the things of the flesh (Rom 8:5).

3 What makes you angry? Are you right to be angry? See Jonah 4.

# 12  THE WORLD OF WORK

I do not think of Christ as God alone, or man alone, but
both together. For I know he was hungry, and I know
that with five loaves he fed 5000 people (St Chrysostom).

Jesus is the Lord of creation and the carpenter of Nazareth.
His feet bestride the universe, and they stood among the
wood shavings and sawdust of Joseph's bench. He
fashioned furniture during his life and he furnished salvation in his death. He is both servant and labourer, and
saviour and Lord. His lordship should affect our work!

## Attitudes towards work

We think of those who earn wages or a salary as 'working',
but not those who stay at home looking after the children.
We appear to have one attitude towards the man who
works in the steel mill with its sweat, dirt and noise, and
another towards the man who reads and studies in a library.

Why do we pay more attention to or think more important the husband who holds a responsible job in the City
than to the devoted mother who drives voluntarily for a
local luncheon club, or visits a shut-in parent?

In the eyes of the world, work is that for which we get
paid. We view work through the eyes of the world rather
than through the eyes of the creator.

If we want to understand the lordship of Jesus towards
the world of work, we must touch on several important
issues: our reasons for working; the root problems of work;
specific issues such as unemployment and unfair dismissal;
boredom; the Christian's attitude to vocation, rest, holidays and retirement, as well as the dangers and rewards of
work.

# Reasons for working

There always have been, and always will be, very different reasons for working.

On the one hand, there are bad or inadequate reasons for work. Some people work merely in order to provide for the material and financial needs of themselves and their families. Some plan to do as little work as possible – just enough to keep their jobs! Yet others, in marked contrast, are workaholics.

On the other hand, there are good reasons for work. We work because work is sharing in and reflecting God's essential work and nature as the creator. We work because it is part of our Christian calling and discipleship. 'Make it your ambition to lead a quiet life, to mind your own business and to work with your hands, just as we told you, so that your daily life may win the respect of outsiders and so that you will not be dependent on anybody' (1 Thess 4:11–12); or 'Serve wholeheartedly, as if you were serving the Lord, not men, because you know that the Lord will reward everyone for whatever good he does, whether he is slave or free' (Eph 6:7–8).

Commenting on this passage, William Barclay has written:

> The conviction of the Christian workman is that every single piece of work he produces must be good enough to show to God . . . The only secret of good workmanship is that it is done for God. It is only when a man is taking all his work and showing it to God that work can be good.[1]

Our Christian calling and discipleship is not only to produce good work for the sake of the work but to produce work that is to the glory of God.

As Jesus taught in the sermon on the mount, our light is to shine before men so that they may see our good deeds and praise our Father in heaven (Mt 5:16). Paul makes a similar point when urging the Corinthians, 'whether you eat or drink or whatever you do, do it all for the glory of God' (1 Cor 10:31).

Parliament is one place that legislates for our work. In the chair of the House of Commons is Mr Speaker – one of the most ancient and honourable of political offices anywhere in the world. Lord Tonypandy, formerly George Thomas, was the Speaker in the early 1980s, and reveals in his autobiography why he wanted to enter Parliament from the background of the coalmining areas of South Wales:

> I wanted to use politics as a means of translating Christian values into practice, for I believed then as I do now, that Parliament is one of the means for Christian people to make the world look like God's world – though I do not believe it is ever right for the church to tell people how to vote.[2]

Christians who acknowledge Jesus as Lord over every sphere of life seek to translate that lordship into every area they are involved in – whether it is politics, business, sport, or intellectual and academic interests.


## The root problem of work

If it were true that we work because God is the creator, that we share the desire to create, and that all work is enjoyable, productive and useful, then life would be very easy. But that, sadly, is not the whole truth. Work and workers have been subject to the fall and the consequent downward pull of sin from the beginning of time.

Sin and Satan have spoilt the world of work. Work has been described as painful:

> There is a deeply rooted element of pain in the human experience of work. Agricultural labouring was until recently hard and relentless. Factory work is still often monotonous, repetitive, meaningless, soul-destroying. Many products are of dubious value, promoted by

excessive advertising. Wants have been turned into needs. There is much waste. Armaments are a major part of the world economy. Much high technology research is related to defence contracts. Stress and pressure cause mental breakdowns and physical illness. Conflict in large organisations seems to be endemic.[3]

God warned Adam about this when he first disobeyed: 'Cursed is the ground because of you; through painful toil you will eat of it all the days of your life' (Gen 3:17).

How can a Christian respond to some of the deep problems and dilemmas that result from work having been marred by sin and spoilt by Satan? Let me suggest a few guidelines, though I realise there are no easy answers to such constant and complex issues.

## The lordship of Christ and unemployment

On the British and world scene, unemployment is here to stay, and sadly it has been an increasing personal problem for many people.

There are four aspects of this problem about which Christians should be deeply concerned. First, *we should be concerned about unemployment itself* and what it means in terms of human misery and personal dignity. Sadly, some Christians eschew political – and party political – matters as if they are no concern of the spiritually-minded Christian. They act as if there is nothing they can do. But work finds its very meaning in the nature of God and the lordship of Christ over his world. There should be no group of people more concerned about unemployment than the Christian church.

Second, *we should be concerned for our area*. A growing number of churches are setting up drop-in centres, training schemes, advice centres, and help of one sort or another to those who are unemployed. The church as a community can offer practical help.

My first curacy was served at St George's, Leeds, famous for the work of its Crypt among down and outs – men and women in need of food, clothing, work, medical and dental care and, above all, human and divine love. A variety of help is offered. There is a workshop where men produce wire coathangers which are sold to dry-cleaning shops. How easy it is to ignore the wire coathanger when we collect our suit or dress from the cleaners! That wire coathanger represents useful work to the man who thought he would never have a job again. His dignity has been recovered through a simple but necessary work. Or again, the residents of a mentally handicapped hospital may not be capable of work as most of us would understand it, but they gain a tremendous sense of achievement through the work of packing basic hospital supplies into boxes.

Third, *we may be called to minister to men and women in our fellowships who have been made redundant* and help them to understand that the lordship of Jesus extends to these circumstances. For a man, especially for the husband, the father and head of the family, being without work starts to undermine his dignity and self-confidence. He begins to question his worth and existence. He finds himself becoming depressed, and tension builds up in the home.

At the heart of the gospel is the fact that the Lord accepts us as we are. Our value does not rest in our work or past achievement, but simply in the fact that God loves us enough for Jesus to die for us. Our true value rests in the Lord Jesus and not in the salary we earn. As men in our own church can testify, times of unemployment can be times of proving, in a deeper way, the care and provision of the living Lord.

Fourth, *every Christian is called to be a responsible citizen of both heaven and earth*. We therefore have the opportunity to influence the political decisions in our country – not only the issues of employment but every other political issue. We are able to canvass Members of Parliament, and if we have the right to vote, then we have the responsibility to vote. I believe we demonstrate the lordship of Christ not by declaring politics a dirty business – it may well be – but by seeking to elect representatives to local councils, to Parliament and to the European Parliament, who will most nearly speak from a Christian position. Paul reminds us that 'the powers that be' are ordained by God. If the lordship of Christ demands we submit to civil authorities and rulers, then his lordship also invites us to use our vote to elect them.

## The lordship of Christ and unfair dismissal

This will be a minor problem to most, but a major issue for those involved in it and for ministers called to advise Christians in this position. We need to know how to operate under the lordship of Christ when unfairly dismissed from work. It is very easy to become resentful and bitter in such circumstances. It is equally easy to act as if this should not concern a Christian, and to assume that there is nothing one should do.

But God is a God of righteousness and justice, and we should be occupied with issues of righteousness and justice as we live under the lordship of Jesus. However, we are not to take vengeance into our own hands. '"It is mine to avenge; I will repay," says the Lord' (Rom 12:19). We are to resist the evil but love the sinner.

We are not to be mindless and uncaring doormats for everyone to wipe their unholy feet on. Nor are we to be indignant and resentful tyrants thirsting for everyone's blood. Rather we are to strive for righteousness without vindictiveness. We may encourage a Christian to clear his or her name and to seek compensation for unfair dismissal, without speaking unkindly of those who have dismissed them. This is not easy, and is often a long and painful process. We acknowledge Jesus' lordship and our solidarity with them by bearing their burdens and taking up their righteous cause.

The psalmist poses the question: 'When the foundations are being destroyed, what can the righteous do?' (Ps 11:3). Too easily we can assume there is nothing we can do. But he continues, 'The Lord is in his holy temple; the Lord is on his heavenly throne. He observes the sons of men . . . the wicked and those who love violence his soul hates . . . For the Lord is righteous, he loves justice' (Ps 11:4–7). We are to be involved on the side of justice and righteousness in the sinful and unjust world of work.

## The lordship of Christ and boredom in work

> Two men looked out from prison bars,
> One saw dust, while the other saw stars.

How you look at a situation, and whether you think positively or negatively, will determine whether you are frustrated or fulfilled. Frankly, there is much that is mundane, routine and boring in many jobs. We may be doing work for which we are overqualified, or to which the Lord is not calling us. Assuming, however, that you are a Christian in a routine job, how do you regard your work? Paul's instructions to the Colossians are still applicable: 'And whatever you do, whether in word or deed, do it all in the name of the Lord Jesus, giving thanks to God the Father through him . . . Whatever you do, work at it with all your heart, as working for the Lord, not for men' (Col 3:17,23).

One housewife has described her answer to the problem of routine work in this way:

It is hard to describe some domestic activities in anything other than negative words and phrases – such as futile, wearing, tiring, will-have-to-be-done-again-tomorrow, frustrating, unfulfilling, unrewarding. Any feelings of pleasure we might feel from seeing crumbs being sucked up by a vacuum cleaner are short-lived, and any sense of satisfaction we might receive at polished glass doors and mirrors and fireplaces, lasts only until the next person pushes through them hands first or the wind drives rubbish down the chimney! Can God really speak to us through this negativity? The answer is 'yes' to both questions, for I am like the crumby floor, the marked glass, the dirty oven, and the dusty shelves. My Father cleans me up, wipes me over again and again and never uses negative words or phrases to describe the process. If my sin is overcome today I may well fall again tomorrow and he will have to mop up once more or dust me down another time, but he does so cheerfully, tirelessly, positively, lovingly and I am left amazed at his patience, resilience, dedication and joy at doing his housework on me.[4]

## *The lordship of Christ and vocation to Christian service*

Many Christians have too narrow a view of their vocation in life. Christian vocation should not be limited to the ordained ministry of the church, missionary service and certain professional callings. It is true that clergy, missionaries and those in 'full-time' Christian service must have a sense of the Lord's calling. But it is equally true that each one of us must know that he is working where the Lord would have him work.

We should end the divide that has existed for too long between the 'secular' and the 'spiritual'. This is not in order to make the spiritual secular, but it is to sanctify the secular. Thus, the lordship of Jesus means that the secretary in the local hospital or the man occupied in the money markets of the world knows that this is where God has called him or her, and in that job they will seek to honour their Lord and master in the work they do and in the life they live.

## Rest and holidays

Work and rest are linked together in the scriptures: 'By the seventh day God had finished the work he had been doing; so on the seventh day he rested from all his work. And God blessed the seventh day and made it holy, because on it he rested from all the work of creating that he had done' (Gen 2:2–3); 'Remember the Sabbath day by keeping it holy. Six days you shall labour and do all your work, but the seventh day is a Sabbath to the Lord your God . . . Therefore the Lord blessed the Sabbath day and made it holy' (Exod 20:8–11).

This insistence upon the essential partnership of work and rest runs through the Old Testament. In the New Testament it is transformed by the resurrection to the first day of the week, but still the pattern of work and rest continues.

At the same time, the pattern needs to extend to holidays. Holidays were once holy days. There were many holy days in the Bible – days of feasting and joy and rest from work in order to rejoice in the goodness of God. We have moved very far from that purpose as society has become more secular and the holiday industry has grown to include travel to far-away places. The Christian is still called to make Jesus Lord of holidays – how they are used, how much money is spent on them, and how this relates to our overall giving. I suspect that many Christians spend more on their holidays than their giving, and this was never the Lord's purpose.

In 1986 Britain saw the debate about the revision of the Sunday trading laws. The arguments put forward to retain Sunday as a special day related to the welfare of the family, the economic issues, the interests of the firm's staff: very rarely did they relate to the first principles of the commandments of the Lord and the lordship of Jesus. This is not to belittle other arguments. For example, it matters profoundly, if Sunday trading laws were revised, that Sunday would become the second-busiest shopping day of the week, that almost a million married women in the retail business would have to work on Sundays or lose their jobs, that small businesses would be forced out of existence, and that more children could be left at home while parents worked. All these issues affect the health and wellbeing of the community. But more important than these is the acknowledgement of the lordship of Jesus and the desire of men and women to obey the commandments.

## The lordship of Jesus and retirement

In the usual course of events, work will end and retirement will begin, and it will come to an increasing number of people. Our older population is growing in numbers – so much so that the Government is having to revise radically security benefits and pension arrangements for the generations that will retire after the year 2035. How we spend our retirement time and devote the freer years of our lives is another area that must come under the lordship of Jesus.[5]

## The rewards and dangers of work

There are many rewards for work, but there are also many dangers. Moses warned God's people about this danger when they came into the promised land:

> When you have eaten and are satisfied, praise the Lord your God for the good land he has given you. Be careful that you do not forget the Lord your God . . . You may say to yourself, 'My power and the strength of my hands have produced this wealth for me.' But remember the Lord your God, for it is he who gives you the ability to produce wealth, and so confirms his covenant . . .
> (Deut 8:10–11,17–18)

Jesus also told the story of the rich fool who rejoiced in his prosperity and harvest, and decided to build larger barns to hold his goods and then sat back and took life easy, forgetting God (Lk 12:13–21). Likewise, there are many warnings throughout the Bible against the subtle dangers of covetousness and greed. Thus, as Christians, we need to be on our guard against the spiritual dangers that surround the rich rewards of work – pride, covetousness, a growing secular and materialistic outlook – and to honour the Lord as the one who has enabled us all the way through. No wonder the writer of the Proverbs reminds us to acknowledge the Lord in all our ways and to 'honour the Lord with your wealth, with the firstfruits of all your crops; then your barns will be filled to overflowing, and your vats will brim over with new wine' (Prov 3:9–10).

How can we honour the Lord with our work and wealth

when we know of millions of mothers who weep because they cannot feed their babies, of millions of families living in the increasing number of 'barrios' or shanty towns around the vast urban areas of the world who are trying to scratch a living from rubbish heaps and waste bins of the world, of vast areas without a health service, or of millions facing the daily threat of famine and starvation – and yet we panic because we cannot live on the average wage of £150 a week in 1986?

## Where do we start?

When and how do we begin to make Jesus Lord of our working world? The answer of the Old Testament bids us to 'Remember your Creator in the days of your youth, before the days of trouble come' (Eccl 12:1); so make Jesus Lord as soon as you can!

The whole of Ecclesiastes is devoted to a man seeking to find a satisfying philosophy in life. He has to conclude that life, pleasure, wealth and work only have their meaning as we remember and acknowledge that God is the creator (Eccl 1:3; 2:10–11,18–23; 3:13; 4:8; 5:15–18; 6:7; 8:15; 9:9; 10:15). Thus the person who acknowledges that Jesus is the Lord of their work discovers fulfilment at school and college, in the home and the shop, in retirement and among the heaviest responsibilities any person may face.

## For personal reflection or group study

1 Are there practical steps your own church can take to ease the problem of unemployment in the local area, or for individual church members?
2 How should parents – and the youth fellowship – help teenagers to have the right attitudes towards school work and future employment?
3 What differences will honouring Jesus as Lord make to your own holiday plans?

# 13 THE PRESSURE OF TIME

'Actually I've discovered the perfect solution to the problem of time!'

Everyone stopped talking and stared at me.

'It's easy,' I said. 'It's changed my life!'

There was a breathless pause.

'I just don't go to any meetings at all!' I sat back and waited. . . .

Thus Jenny Cooke writes about the frantic church.[1] All of us would share her problem about time, many of us would long to have the courage to adopt her radical solution and few probably feel they are master of their time. Instead of being able to live life calmly, with the attitude that Jesus is Lord of our time, we work anxiously through many responsibilities, praying, 'Lord, more time please.'

Surely something is wrong somewhere. The familiar story of Martha and Mary may help us. The account in Luke 10:38–42 is well known. Jesus came to stay with the two sisters in their home at Nazareth. It was Martha – the elder sister? – who invited him in, but she was under pressure, being pulled frantically in all directions at once, while Mary, who had helped Martha with the preparations, had time to sit at Jesus' feet and listen to his teaching. What was the vital difference? It lies in the fact that Martha was concerned with *her* programme, plans and agenda, while Mary was concerned with the agenda and planning of *her Lord*. For Martha it was a matter of her time; for Mary it was Jesus' time.

## What is time?

We must remember that life in Bible times was lived without all the present-day measures of time! There were no diaries, calendars, watches and clocks, and no speaking clock giving the accurate time every ten seconds. Instead, in the Old Testament, men were governed by God-given, rather than man-made measurements of time – the seasons, the sun and the moon, the stars, the sabbaths. In the New Testament there would be the great annual festivals and the use of the Jewish calendar.[2]

Everyone has the same amount of time, yet for some it flies and for others it hangs heavily. For some there is not enough; for others there is too much. What matters about time is how we regard it and how we use it. So how should we view time once we have made Jesus Lord, and what might this mean in practical daily living?

## The right view of time

Various Greek words are used which we translate into English as 'time'. There is *hora* – which means hour. Something happens at the third or sixth or ninth hour of the day. It is a precise timing. There is *chronos* – which means a specific event or time, as, for example, when the disciples asked Jesus: 'Lord, are you at this time going to restore the kingdom to Israel?' and he replied: 'It is not for you to know the times or dates the Father has set by his own authority' (Acts 1:6–7). A third word is *kairos*, which means an opportunity – 'Therefore, as we have opportunity, let us do good to all people' (Gal 6:10).

We can begin to see from these three different words that time may be a definite opportunity, a specific time in the future or an exact hour on a certain day now. They remind us that God, even though he is eternal, is concerned with time. Because of this we need to have the right perspective on time and history.

We shall examine three inadequate attitudes to time before turning to consider what the Christian's view of time ideally should be.

## Wrong and inadequate views of time

*Too long a view of time.* We can be those who will happily put off until tomorrow what we don't have to do today. There is no sense of urgency. We are like the housewife who plans to put all the loose recipes she has collected together into some order for easy reference, but won't do it now, and then spends half an hour looking for one special recipe when she is pressed for time to get supper!

*Too short a view of time.* While we are impatiently and anxiously concerned with now, and the present minute, God is concerned with generations and eternity. It is fascinating to read in Psalm 90 that man is occupied with days, but God is taken up with generations. The Lord has an overall view of time, and he is in no hurry.

Consider the many Christian parents who pray faithfully for the conversion of their children. The son who rebelled at sixteen may be training for the ministry and utterly committed to the Lord by the time he is twenty-five. We can have too short a view of time.

*Too weak a view of time.* Jesus is the Alpha and the Omega, the beginning and the end (Rev 1:8,17; cf. Col 1:15). God sees the end from the beginning and he knows how events will turn out. Birth and death are the entry and exit points for eternity. God is much bigger than our view of time and history. We may view the moral and spiritual state of nations with alarm, and wonder what on earth the world is coming to, but God has the overall view.

Most of us fall into these traps about time – we are either too careless about time, too impatient about time, or too short-sighted to see the Lord working his purposes out. What then is the right attitude to time?

## The Christian view of time

*Time is God-given.* It has been that way from the beginning, when God made the sun and the moon, caused there

to be day and night and created light and darkness. We are
living in God's time, not ours. Thus we are to be stewards of
time, not owners of time.

One young mother wrote to me about her problem and
attitude to time.

> I had a whole sphere of new responsibilities which were
> somewhat bewildering and time consuming. Prayer time
> vanished in the multitude of other things to be done in
> the limited time available. The Lord then showed me the
> answer. As soon as my son went to sleep in the morning, I
> was to have a time of quiet with God. At first this seemed
> the ultimate sacrifice of time, but the Lord helped me to
> be disciplined and not feel tempted into doing little
> things first, and it very soon became a time of great
> blessing to me. It also had a side effect – almost invari-
> ably the other jobs got done as well and I noticed that on
> the few days when I missed that time of quiet the day
> never seemed to go smoothly and jobs were often left
> undone.

That mum was only proving the truth of Jesus' promises –
'seek first his kingdom and his righteousness, and all these
things will be given to you as well' (Mt 6:33).

An older person comes to regard each new day as a gift
and a bonus. Those who have lived their three score years
and ten also live with the thought of 'Three score years . . .
and then?' One retired businessman who found he had time
to enjoy his hobbies always cleared his workbench each
evening. 'My bench is tidy – there may not be tomorrow for
me.'

*Time is given to fulfil the calling of God.* As in all things,
Jesus is our great example. Running through John's gospel
is the refrain 'My hour' (e.g. 'My hour has not yet come',
which changes, as he approaches the cross, to 'My hour has
come').

At the same time, Jesus was aware that he had work to do
that had been given by God: 'My food is to do the will of

him who sent me and to finish his work'; 'As long as it is day, we must do the work of him who sent me. Night is coming, when no-one can work'; 'I have brought you glory on earth by completing the work you gave me to do' (Jn 4:34; 9:4; 17:4).

Thus, the man or woman who has made Jesus Lord of their lives and of their time is seeking to be occupied with the work that Jesus would have them to do. The work will be different for us all; it will vary in its character and in its quantity. The Lord will know that some are able to do more or less than others. He knows our capacities. The important thing is that we are not comparing what we do with others, so much as comparing what we do with what the Father plans we should do.

*Time is given for both work and rest.* The lordship of Jesus will affect our work and also our rest, our worship and our holidays.

Too many men, especially, have breakdowns or develop ulcers simply because they disobey the Lord about the use of work time and rest time. Likewise, I am sure that though a woman's work is never done, she should stop and rest. It is a contradiction in terms – as well as in reality – for a woman to be house proud and always 'on the go', and still claim that Jesus is Lord. She may think that is true in her mind, but in fact she is bowing down to the idol of 'her home' and becoming its slave.

*Time has been corrupted by sin.* Satan seeks to make us misuse time. Hence, we are exhorted to redeem time because the days are evil (Eph 5:16). How might we misuse time? We can waste it! How much time is thrown away because we are taken up with things that God does not intend us to do?

We know the unspoken cries of many lives: 'Has anyone seen my time?', 'I haven't got time', etc. Most of us need practical guidelines.

## Some practical guidelines

*Trust the Lord at all times.* 'Trust in him at all times, O people; pour out your hearts to him, for God is our refuge' (Ps 62:8). Unexpected circumstances can arise that threaten to blow our day apart: a train missed because of heavy traffic when we had not allowed extra time, the urgent visitor who calls, the unexpected problem that meant the work took two hours instead of ten minutes – the situations could be multiplied endlessly. The Christian who has committed his time to the Lord and planned ahead as best as he knows how has to trust the Lord to work things out for him.

*Determine and fix your personal priorities.* There is a world of difference between 'what we could do' and 'what we are aiming at'. If we are clear on our aims and priorities, then almost certainly we shall achieve them, together with satisfaction and effectiveness. The prayer: 'Lord, what do you want me to do?' needs to be offered before we plan to use our time.

*Start planning.* For years in the ministry I have used a weekly schedule – a single sheet of paper on my desk indicating the morning, afternoon and evening of each weekday. And before each week begins – sometimes two or three weeks beforehand – I will use that sheet for planning ahead.

As well as adequate forward planning, I try to plan more for the beginning of a week than towards the end so that as extra things crop up or unexpected needs arise I am perfectly able to fit them in. I try to make a distinction between the urgent and the important, to ensure that the important gets done. Where I can delegate I will do so, where I have difficult work to be done, or problems to solve, I will try to tackle them first thing in the morning, when I am at my best. As has been said: 'Plan your work and work your plan.' Planning will also include knowing how to 'stop the leaks'.

*Stop the leaks.* All of us have 168 hours a week – no more and no less. Yet there is a great difference in the ways that time is used. It is often salutary to work out how you spend those 168 hours. What time do you spend sleeping, working, eating, in leisure, devotionally, with the family, etc? When most people do such a stock-taking exercise, they are left asking, 'What do I do with the remaining twenty hours or so?' Lots of little leaks add up to a lot of time that can be redeemed. How? The same jobs waiting to be done, the next few pages of a book waiting to be read, that letter needing to be found, those weeds in the garden. We can plan to stop the leaks and use time as a servant without falling into the trap of making time our master and we its slave.

*Cultivate a quiet spirit.* 'In repentance and rest is your salvation, in quietness and trust is your strength, but you would have none of it' (Isa 30:15).

The Lord himself knew the value of times of strategic withdrawal from the company of people and the pressure of the work in order that he might have time with the Father. He deliberately withdrew in order that he might be renewed. He would allow the Father, rather than the world, to set the pace.

There is a beautiful modern version of Psalm 23 written by a Japanese writer, Tokio Megashie, which aptly sums up our needs:

> The Lord is my Pace setter – I shall not rush.
> He makes me stop for quiet intervals,
> He provides me with images of stillness which restore
>         my serenity,
> He leads me in ways of efficiency through calmness of
>         mind,
>         And his guidance is peace.
> Even though I have a great many things to
>         accomplish each day, I will not fret,
>             for His Presence is here,

His timelessness, His all importance, will keep me in
　　balance.
He prepares refreshment and renewal in the midst of
　　my activity,
By anointing my mind with His oils of tranquillity,
　　My cup of joyous energy overflows.
Truly harmony and effectiveness shall be the fruits of
　　my hours,
For I shall walk in the Pace of my Lord
　　And dwell in His House for ever.

*Recognise the value of time.* One of the great temptations
with time is to compare what one person achieves in their
day with what we achieve in our day. We may feel we are
doing well compared to some people, and rather badly
compared to others.

It is too easy to conclude that we are unprofitable servants when we consider what we have left undone. But the
perspective that gives value to time is whether we are
occupied with what the Lord has called us to do. One
person's time will be taken up with caring for elderly
parents or young children; many will be fully engaged in the
work God has called them to; the wife and mother, whose
children have grown up and left home, will ask the Lord
how he wants her to use time; for the retired, elderly
person, time will have a different value. We must not
compare ourselves with each other; instead we should be
concerned to fill our available time with the programme the
Lord has for us.

*Admit that time will come to an end.* We do not have 'all the
time in the world'. It was the psalmist who wrote, 'Show
me, O Lord, my life's end and the number of my days; let
me know how fleeting is my life. You have made my days a
mere handbreath; the span of my years is as nothing before
you. Each man's life is but a breath' (Ps 39:4–5). At some
points in life we feel permanent and secure. We neither
look back to birth nor look forward to death. But just as
time began for each of us, so time will close for each one –

unless the Lord returns first. One aspect of the lordship of Jesus is acknowledging this truth. Thus we have to be ready to meet the Lord. For everyone, that means that we must be right with him through Jesus and know that our assurance of eternal life rests not in the life we have lived and the works we have done but in the death that he died and the gift of eternal life that he offers to us.

This vital issue is well expressed by a verse written around one of the windows in Chester Cathedral, but here adapted to ask the question: Will I have accepted Christ as my saviour by then?

> When as a child I laughed and wept,
> > Time crept,
> When as a youth I dreamed and talked,
> > Time walked,
> When I became a full grown man,
> > Time ran,
> And later as I older grew,
> > Time flew,
> Soon I shall find, while travelling on,
> > Time gone,
> Will I have accepted Christ as my saviour by then?
> > Amen.

God's purposes for the use of our time and his perspective on time are summed up for us in the Advent Sunday collect in the Church of England's *Alternative Service Book*:

> Almighty God, give us grace to cast away the works of darkness and to put on the armour of light, now in the time of this mortal life, in which your Son Jesus Christ came to us in great humility: so that on the last day, when he shall come again in his glorious majesty to judge the living and the dead, we may rise to the life immortal; through him who is alive and reigns with you and the Holy Spirit, one God, now and for ever.[3]

The lordship of Jesus will mean that we shall restore to our thinking those two missing letters: DV (*Deo volente* –

'God willing') and submit the use of our time to his guidance. It is when we are using our time as the Lord directs us, that we find his time used for our blessing.

## For personal reflection or group study

1 You have been given 168 hours every week. Work out how you use them. What changes would you make under the lordship of Jesus?

2 Discuss the advice you would give a) to the very organised person who doesn't seem to have time to stop and chat and b) to the disorganised person who is always trying to catch up with themselves.

3 For younger people: Have you considered the way you use your leisure time since you became a Christian?
For older people: What plans are you making now about rightly using your retirement time?

# 14   DANGER! MONEY

'There are three conversions necessary: the conversion of the heart, mind, and the purse.'[1] Martin Luther's comment has often been quoted, and it reveals that Christianity affects our use of money. Jesus spoke frequently about it: 'from the parable of the sower to the parable of the rich farmer, from the encounter with the rich young ruler to Zacchaeus, from teachings on trust in Matthew 6 to teachings on the danger of wealth in Luke 6'.[2]

Christians can't live without money, and many can't live with it.

## The basic attitude – stewardship or ownership

Do I own money or does money own me? Do I control money or does money control me? These are some of the simple but searching issues that every Christian needs to face. But before we answer the question about stewardship or ownership, we have to ask a prior question about the nature of money.

## *What is money?*

To claim that 'money is the root of all evil', as the old song goes, or that money is neutral and we use it rightly or wrongly, finds us guilty of misquoting the Bible and mis-understanding the nature of money. Paul wrote: 'The *love* of money is a root of all kinds of evil. Some people, eager for money, have wandered from the faith and pierced themselves with many griefs' (1 Tim 6:10). Richard Foster makes the very important point, in *Money*, *Sex and Power*, that money not only has a light side which is good, it also has a dark side which can control us.[3]

Jesus taught that we cannot serve two masters: either we will hate the one and serve the other, or we will be devoted to the one and despise the other (Mt 6:24).

Therefore, the Christian who would live under the lordship of Jesus not only has to recognise the real nature of money but also has to acknowledge that God is the rightful owner of money and wealth and possessions, and that he – the disciple – is the steward.

## God is the rightful owner

The psalmist proclaims that 'The earth is the Lord's, and everything in it' (Ps 24:1; cf. Ps 50:9–12). In various parts of the scriptures we are called upon to be the faithful stewards of God's world and its resources in general, and the goods that God has entrusted to us as individuals in particular (Ps 8:6–8; Deut 8:11–20; Lev 25:23; Lk 12:48). We have no absolute right to possess anything, since there is only one ultimate owner – God.

Thus God's ownership of all things actually enhances our relationship with him. When we truly know that the earth is the Lord's, then property itself makes us more aware of God.[4] This frees us from a possessive and anxious spirit.

## Covetousness or contentment

Just as we have to choose, in our basic attitude, between seeing God as owner and man as steward or seeing God as creator and man as owner, so we have a fundamental choice in our approach to money between one of getting or giving, between covetousness or contentment.

There are very many warnings in the scriptures about the subtle and growing dangers of covetousness (Exod 20:17; Josh 7:21; Eph 5:3; 1 Tim 6:10). We need to see the essential difference between *using* money (or mammon) and *serving* money. We need instruction on how to possess money without being possessed by money.[5]

The original Hebrew and Greek words of the Bible that we translate as 'covetous' actually mean: to desire for oneself, to gain unlawfully or dishonestly, to wish for more, to extend the arms for anything, to love silver.

We need to recognise and admit that as Christians we live in a fallen and covetous world that seeks its own, and seeks to bring Christians down to its own standards. Christians come to expect the usual annual salary and wage increase. We assume that our standard of living should rise year after year, that our holidays should become more and more exciting. We believe the worldly and enticing advertising all around us. Yesterday's luxuries have become today's necessities. Christians are not free from these subtle and powerful pressures.

The Christian alternative to a covetous spirit is the Spirit of contentment. That does not necessarily mean poverty, as Paul writes: 'I have learned to be content whatever the circumstances. I know what it is to be in need, and I know what it is to have plenty. I have learned the secret of being content in any and every situation, whether well fed or hungry, whether living in plenty or in want. I can do everything through him who gives me strength' (Phil 4:11–13).

Often our burdens and worries are financial and material ones. Frequently the tensions and arguments that arise within a marriage are focused on money. So it is clearly very important that we discover the secret of contentment.

The heart of contentment lies in the contentment of the heart, and the secret of this is found in our Christian faith.

First, it is found in the right world-view and perspective on life. It is very uneasy and uncomfortable to be living in two worlds at once. As Christians, we are to live in this world, but we are to have our eyes clearly focused on the world to come. Thus our security and values do not rest in the things of this world, which is passing, but in the lasting world to come.

Second, we can have contentment without conformity to this world. It is desperately easy to think that security, meaning and acceptance are found in living as our non-Christian friends do. Our contentment is to be found in

Christ rather than through resting in our status and possessions in the world.

Third, we can be content in the present moment because we know that the Lord will provide for the future as we seek first his kingdom, rule and righteousness. So many modern-day concerns are focused upon providing for the future – large pension investments, massive insurance schemes to counter inflation, money put away for a rainy day, things we hope to do when 'our ship comes in'. I am not asking that we are careless and irresponsible in these matters. We do have duties laid upon us by the scriptures to provide for our families, and we are commanded to be wise. We are, however, commanded not to be over-anxious or to fret about the future or to be so overcommitted financially that we are not able to be wise stewards of all God gives us. The clear teaching of scripture is that as we are responsible about the Lord's concerns, so he will be careful about ours. Or as Paul wrote to the Philippians: 'My God will meet all your needs according to his glorious riches in Christ Jesus' (Phil 4:19).

## The call to simplicity

Such a promise should promote confidence in life, and it can also result, as Richard Foster points out, in simplicity of life: 'We who follow Jesus Christ are called to a vow of simplicity . . . All who name Christ as Lord and Saviour are obliged to follow what he says, and Jesus' call to disciple-ship in money can be best summed up in the single word *simplicity*. Simplicity seeks to do justice to our Lord's many-faceted teachings about money . . .'[6]

We have already noted that Jesus taught about simplicity – or singleness of purpose – in the sermon on the mount. St Paul taught the same. In Romans 12:8 he calls us to share with others and do it *generously* (GNB). The NIV also trans-lates the Greek word by 'generously', the RSV says, 'with liberality', and the AV uses the key word, 'simplicity'.

Thus as we make Jesus Lord and respond to him with

singleness of mind and heart, so our giving will be marked out by liberality and generosity.

## Simplicity will lead to generosity

Generosity is more a matter of the human spirit than the huge sum given. Consider, for a few moments, the widow whose giving Jesus commended (Mk 12:41–44).

Jesus saw three groups of people gathered together in the temple courts. In the court of the women were thirteen collecting boxes called 'the trumpets' into which people would place their offerings for various needs. Jesus saw the multitude. He noticed that many rich people threw in large amounts. But then he spotted a widow who put in two very small copper coins. She gave all she had.

This incident is a picture of our giving within the Christian church. All will give some, many will give much, but few give all. Jesus did not judge the giving of the multitude and the many. But he gladly commended the giving of the widow, and in so doing appeared to get his arithmetic wrong. She had put in so little, yet Jesus remarked that, 'They all gave out of their wealth; but she, out of her poverty, put in everything – all she had to live on' (v.44). Jesus commended her because he saw the heart of the giver rather than the size of the gift. She gave from a generous and sacrificial spirit.

For us, sacrificial giving is allowing the Lord to do what he wills with our possessions, savings, trust funds, investments, stocks and shares, deposit accounts, building society funds, special deposit accounts as well as our wages and salary and unemployment benefit.

It is often Christians in the third world who have learnt this lesson first. They will give their guests the last egg, and go without themselves, though hungry. They will give and not count the cost because this was the way the master gave. They know that it is more blessed to give than to receive (Acts 20:35). Giving, for them, is not so much an activity when the collection is being taken up, but an attitude that characterises their lives – they go on giving whether it is with their money, their possessions, their time, their hearts or their love. They demonstrate the fact that when Jesus changes a person, he changes them radically from the inside out, and instead of demanding to get, get, get, their desire is to give, give, give.

## The results of giving

There are a number of results from true Christian giving – glory will be brought to the Lord, the needs of individuals and churches and Christian work will be met, we shall have spiritual blessings and we shall find that as we give, so God will go on giving to us. I want to concentrate upon these last two results of giving.

*We shall go on receiving.* Jesus expounded the truth: 'Give, and it will be given to you. A good measure, pressed down, shaken together and running over, will be poured into your lap. For with the measure you use, it will be measured to you' (Lk 6:38). This is true. But it is to be the result of our giving, not the reason for our giving – otherwise covetousness has entered into our hearts.

But we need to be on our guard against the modern cult of the prosperity teachers of the western world. They remind us that God promises us all we need, that we have only to claim by faith what we need and God will answer, and that material blessing is a sign of God's direct favour. Such prosperity teaching is too simplistic and deceptive. It does not do honour to the Lord, and it falls down at a number of very important points.

It fails to recognise the sinfulness of the human heart and the real danger of covetousness in our personal motives. It neglects the fact that money is not neutral, but as we yield to it, so we become subject to it. It ignores the fact of the third world and its appalling starvation and famine and material needs, often due to national and international economic and ecological factors, and it side-steps the fact that God is sovereign.

*There will be spiritual blessing.* There is a vital link between generous giving and spiritual power (Acts 4:32–37). History teaches us that the materially impoverished third world often displays a spiritual power that the materially rich western world cannot emulate.

## Something to remember

Money is a very practical matter, but it is also a very spiritual one, and needs to be submitted to the lordship of Jesus, as does every other area of our lives. It is associated with such words as stewardship, contentment and simplicity. Our attitude to it will affect our giving and lifestyle. It links our inner hidden life with our outward daily living.

## For personal reflection or group study

1 What dangers do you find that money – or the lack of it – brings to both your fellowship and your family?
2 How can the fact that Jesus is Lord help you face the change you feel you should adopt in your attitude to and use of money?
3 What practical steps does your church need to take to help people give in a way that honours the Lord?

# 15  HOME IS HIS CASTLE

It is said that an Englishman's home is his castle. But the lordship of Christ requires that our home becomes *his* castle.

This truth dawned upon my wife and myself at almost the same time. We stood talking in the kitchen, when suddenly we both realised we had not actually and outwardly made Jesus Lord of our home.

We had rejoiced that Jesus was Lord of the church, and we had worked our way through making him Lord of every part of the church's life and head of each group in the church – something that we find we need constantly to affirm. I had often preached and taught that Jesus demanded to be made Lord of every individual Christian's life, but we had been blind to the fact that we hadn't consciously affirmed his lordship together as husband and wife. We knew we had both done so in our hearts and minds and wills, but until that moment we hadn't spoken it out loud.

What does it mean, and what can it mean for a family and for an individual, to submit to the lordship of Jesus in their home and private life? Let me tackle some of the major aspects in this final chapter.

## The position we occupy

We are either single, married, divorced or widowed, and often those who are on their own – for whatever reason – find it hard when the church's programme seems to stress the 'family' aspect of life. There are family services, events for Mother's Day (and in some churches for Father's Day) and there is an emphasis on the family at times like Christmas and Easter, so it is not surprising that the man or woman on their own finds this very difficult.

In return, the people with family responsibilities can sometimes envy the greater freedom of single people who are free of family ties to go off to special events, conferences, or just to travel.

It is clear that each situation has its advantages and disadvantages, but it is essential that we regard our position in life as the one to which the Lord has called us, and not one against which we rebel. When in 1 Corinthians 7 Paul wrote to various categories of people – the married, the unmarried and the widows – on the subject of marriage, he stated a preference: 'I wish that all men were as I am. But each man has his own gift from God; one has this gift, another has that' (1 Cor 7:7). But he also lays down an important principle: 'Nevertheless, each one should retain the place in life that the Lord assigned to him and to which God has called him' (1 Cor 7:17).

Jesus has called us to our different situations, so we must never regard people as first- or second-class citizens, depending on their marital status. Nor must we fall into the trap of thinking that only married people can consecrate their homes to the Lord. There are many homes of single or widowed people that reflect the lordship of Jesus and are truly a foretaste of heaven here on earth.


## The person we marry

The desire that most people have to be married is very natural and very strong, but it is a desire that Satan can prostitute – as he has everything else. Too often, Christians ignore the plain and persistent teaching of both the Old and New Testament about marrying 'in the Lord' – that is marrying someone with the same commitment to the Lord Jesus as themselves. This unchanging injunction – not to be yoked together with unbelievers – is given by St Paul in 2 Corinthians 6:14. Yet there are still Christian girls or young men in every generation who feel that they are an exception, or that they will still honour the Lord and win their partner to Christ, and who go ahead and marry, but not in the Lord.

Twenty-five years' observation of this situation leads me to three conclusions. First, the partnership will only work as a Christian marriage if the other partner becomes a committed Christian before the marriage and not afterwards.

Second, the temptation to disobey the Lord at this point is greater now than ever before because of the imbalance of the sexes within our church fellowships – how often a young woman looks around a congregation and sighs: 'Where are the Christian young men from among whom I might find a life-partner?'

Third, the Christian partner will fall away from the Lord sooner or later, pulled down by wife or husband, unless he or she has made very clear from the beginning that they intend to maintain their commitment to Jesus – incomplete as it is through this marriage of disobedience.

## A biblical principle

While Christians are to marry only in the Lord, what does the lordship of Jesus mean in a marriage where neither were Christians at the time of the wedding, but one has since been converted? This was as frequent a pastoral situation for the early church as it is now, and Peter writes very clearly in 1 Peter 3:1–8 about the reaction of wife to husband and vice versa.

The remarkable fact that many an unbelieving husband finds difficult to understand – but he nevertheless likes the problem – is that his wife has changed for the better! She is more understanding, seeks to submit to him, does not nag him too often about coming to church, has a growing love for him, and generally is a more contented person to live with. He even finds himself thinking that if Christianity – or church – can do that for his wife, maybe there is something in it for him!

## The foundations

Many have been the sermons preached and books written about the foundations of a happy home and family life. Billy Graham, for example, has stressed the following six essentials of a happy home:

  i. It is founded on a divinely ordered marriage.
 ii. It is founded on prayer and Bible reading.
iii. It requires a dedicated husband and father.
 iv. It requires a devoted wife and mother.
  v. It should have disciplined and obedient children.
 vi. It is founded on commitment to Jesus Christ.

That last point is the heart of the matter. Writing to the church at Ephesus about marriage and the husband-wife relationship, Paul summed it all up in the phrase: 'As Christ' (see Eph 5:23,25,29). Jesus is to be both the pattern and the inspiration for every marriage. His relationship with the church is to inspire the relationship between husband and wife. His love for the church is to be the model of the love of husband for wife. His purpose in dying for the church is to be the incentive for the holiness and harmony between wife and husband. His care for his bride is to be matched by the husband's care of his life partner. But Jesus not only provided the pattern, he released the power of his Spirit to make it possible.

## A biblical example

Because marriage can be such a blessing, it is essential to find the right partner. This is the longing not only of young people but also of their Christian parents. But it is sometimes not at all easy. It was the concern of Abraham, too, on behalf of his son Isaac. The events recorded in Genesis 24 illustrate some of the unchanging principles involved when Jesus is head over our own marriages and homes, and also over the future homes and marriages of the younger generation.

There are four key ideas to note in this beautiful and tender account.

*The condition.* Abraham had to look for a wife for Isaac from among his own people, and not from among the Canaanites among whom they were living (Gen 24:3–4, 27–38). Here is the biblical pattern of marriage 'in the Lord' which we also have recorded in 1 Corinthians 7:39.

*The confirmation.* Abraham sent his servant to find a wife, but the servant's task was not to make the choice, rather it was to recognise the woman whom the Lord was bringing to Isaac. There could well have been a number of possible wives for Abraham's son, but the key was recognising the one whom the Lord had chosen (see Gen 24:12–14). If this was to happen, the servant had to remain walking and living in the path of the Lord. It is never too early for parents to be praying for their children's future partners, and to pray that they will recognise the one whom the Lord is drawing to them.

*The compatibility.* The account reveals Rebecca's character very clearly. We read about her physical appearance (Gen 24:16), her social background (Gen 24:15), her emotional stability (Gen 24:58). Her caring and generous personality is seen (Gen 24:14,25). God was calling two people who would be personally, emotionally, socially and spiritually compatible with each other. It is usually not sufficient for two people to be Christians. They should have more in common than their faith.

*The confidence.* There is a thread of confidence that the Lord will guide and provide running throughout the story (Gen 24:40,42,48,50,56,60). Here is the key for parents and children to hold to through all the testing times they may face.

## The responsibilities we have

Marriage in the Lord leads us to new responsibilities towards our life partners, to our children, to our parents and to the institution of marriage itself.

## *Responsibilities to our life partner*

It is unrealistic to assume that every Christian husband and wife find this easy to work out. For most there are growing pains and crises. Paul Yonggi Cho, the Korean pastor, had to learn the hard way.

He taught and lived that his first priority was to the Lord and that the second was to himself. His third was to his wife and the fourth would be to any children God gave them.

> Patiently the Lord explained to Yonggi Cho how fundamental are marriage relationships. What testimony would he have if his wife were to leave him and he ended up divorced? He was to love her as Christ loved the church, to give her fellowship and make her secure. His fifth priority, after the family, was the church, a complete reversal of thinking.

Yonggi Cho needed to make some changes in his life if he was to honour his wife and family.

> Out came his diary and many evangelistic campaigns were cancelled. God said to him, 'Give every Monday to your wife.' So began a new lifestyle. 'Whatever you want to do today, we'll do.'
>
> More than being a dutiful husband, he was obeying the Lord and it was not all that easy. In fact, at times he was utterly frustrated. They visited the shops until his feet ached, idled in the park on fine days, or perhaps had a meal out. Half the time he was gently boiling inside thinking of all the things he could be doing. However, practising tender loving words with a splash of appreciation spiced their life and soon transformed his wife, and the painful lessons learnt were never forsaken. Even today with the enormous demands upon his time, Monday is the day off for himself and all his staff.[1]

For all of us it takes time to work out our marriage relationships in practice in the Lord.

It takes time to discover the full implications of the

God-given roles of husband and wife. 'God did not make human beings, but created us male and female.'[2] Within that relationship we are to discover the factors of equality, complementarity and responsibility. Thus there is no room in a marriage for superiority, domination or control. As Smith Wrigglesworth's wife replied to him on one occasion: 'You are my husband, but Christ is my Master.'

The roles of husband and wife in the Lord are complementary. 'Equality of worth is not identity of role.' Matthew Henry has put this clearly and quaintly: 'Woman was not made out of his head to top him, nor out of his feet to be trampled upon by him, but out of his side to be equal with him, under his arm to be protected, and near his heart to be beloved.'

Husband and wife each bring their different gifts, personalities, natures and understanding to a marriage, and as each is able to contribute fully, so the marriage relationship and partnership is constantly enriched.

## Responsibilities to our children

There are many books that deal with this vital matter.[3] I want to make just two points here.

The Bible's stress is upon the role of the *father* in bringing up the children. In many Christian homes, however, the father is out most evenings or is back late from work, so the special quality of fatherly love and concern is missing. In contrast to this, it is important to note that Jesus was very aware of his relationship with his father. Maybe the lack of Christian sons and future marriageable men that we have already noted can be traced back to the absence of fatherly influence in earlier years when it mattered. The clear teaching of the New Testament is that fathers are to bring their children up in the fear and admonition of the Lord (Eph 6:4). The spiritual lead in the family is to come from father.

The lordship of Christ should result in the role of the father being taken much more seriously in all its aspects.

The second area I want to comment upon is how

Christians who do not have children react to this under the lordship of Christ. Some couples prayerfully and sacrificially decide not to have a family for the sake of their work and ministry. Other couples eventually have a family of their own after much trial and tribulation, many tests and countless disappointments. They bear testimony to the gift of children as a clear answer to prayer.

Others feel that God is calling them to adopt children into their family, either to complete their natural family or in place of their natural family. Christian parents who adopt know that under the lordship of Jesus any special problems they face and emotional needs that arise will be met through Christ.

But there still remains the heart-rending problem of barrenness for a Christian couple. How should they react to this in the Lord? There are several biblical references to barrenness (e.g. Gen 11:30; 25:21; 29:31; Judg 13:2–3; Isa 54:1; Lk 1:7; 23:29, etc.).

'Barrenness was regarded in the East, not only as a matter of regret, but as a reproach which could lead to divorce . . . It was believed that the gift of children or the withholding of them indicated God's blessing or curse . . .'[4] It would seem that the more accurate view of the Bible's teaching is that the gift of children is a blessing, but that it is not correct to make the corresponding assumption that barrenness is therefore a clear sign of the Lord's judgement. Spiritual factors do not always suggest this, medical understanding can often help, and the scriptures plainly show us that the Lord rejoices when childlessness is ended.

Therefore a couple faced with the difficulty of having their own children must free themselves from any sense of God's curse, and their friends and family must love them with tender understanding. The couple themselves may well find that prayerful and practical persistence results in the delightful words of a future mother: 'I think I'm pregnant.'

## Responsibilities to our parents

The New Testament makes this responsibility clear (e.g. 1 Tim 5:8). It may seem strange to stress this responsibility, but as a nation Britain faces a growing number of older parents – either together or as a surviving father or mother. The average age of the population is rising all the time. The needs of old age continue. Problems of frailty of body, dimness of eyesight and difficulties with hearing all produce their own frustrations and demands. How easy it is for a son or daughter, caught up with their own family and work and life, to sit light to the call of aged parents. Other societies in the world – for example in Pakistan or in Africa with the extended family – care lovingly for such honoured members of society, and we should do no less in the name of the Lord.

## Responsibility to the institution of marriage itself

Sadly, we all are aware that two in five marriages end in divorce and that Christians are not exempt from marriage breakdown. Under the lordship of Jesus we are called to honour him in two clear ways. First, we are to do all we can to prepare couples who are planning to be married. More and more churches are taking time to prepare engaged couples more fully. The second area is the very painful area of the break-up of Christian marriages and the contemplation of divorce where both partners are Christians. The topic of divorce is one on which all Christians do not come to the same conclusions. Some believe that it is not right to enter into divorce, others believe that if there is a divorce, then there should not be the possibility of a remarriage, and still others believe the Bible allows divorce on certain grounds only and that a remarriage is permissible.[5]

## What about the blessings?

We must not only stress the responsibilities in marriage and be aware of the difficulties that some couples encounter, but we must also rejoice in the blessings – and there are many – that we can enjoy under the headship of Jesus.

*Companionship*. The three reasons for marriage in the traditional Prayer Book service listed them in this order: 'It was ordained for the procreation of children . . . It was ordained for a remedy against sin, and to avoid fornication . . . It was ordained for the mutual society, help and comfort that the one ought to have of the other . . .'[6] How much better – and more positive – is the same purpose stated in the new wedding service of the *Alternative Service Book*:

> Marriage is given, that husband and wife may comfort and help each other, living faithfully together in need and in plenty, in sorrow and in joy. It is given, that with delight and tenderness they may know each other in love, and, through the joy of their bodily union, may strengthen the union of their hearts and lives. It is given, that they may have children and be blessed in caring for them and bringing them up in accordance with God's will, to his praise and glory.[7]

From the start God knew that it was not good for man to be alone. Marriage enriched by Christ affords many blessings included in that one word 'companionship'.

*Support in the spiritual battle*. Peter counsels husband and wife to live considerately together and for husbands to treat their wives with respect, so that nothing will hinder their prayers (1 Pet 3:7). Every Christian couple will know the reality of the spiritual battle within marriage – whether it is from within our own hearts, focused upon our children or expressed within society. Under the headship of Jesus, we are bound to face the foe, and 'Though one may be overpowered, two can defend themselves. A cord of three strands is not quickly broken' (Eccl 4:12).

*Opportunity in Christian service*. There is much mention made in the Bible of the use of the home. While not every married couple has either the gift for or the opportunity of hospitality, there is a joy in serving the Lord together, whether in the home or the church or the community. We encourage, support, stimulate and at times correct one another.

*The privilege and gift of children.* Children have been described variously as 'little angels' and 'little devils', depending upon the attitude of their parents and the activities of the children concerned.

As the children grow up and reach their teens, most families pass through times of tension and anxiety. Parents are thankful that 'teenagerhood' does not last for ever. Teenagers see a light at the end of the tunnel, realising that they will not be under their parents' eye all the time! It is in the nitty-gritty, cut and thrust of everyday issues – such as who uses the phone next, or which programme you watch on TV – that the reality of the headship and lordship and life of Jesus is seen – or not seen.

It is at times like this that both parents and children need to recall how important each is to the other, and both to the Lord. Many have been the children from Christian homes who have caught what it means to have Jesus as Lord, and have gone on to establish their own homes and witness and effective Christian lives for the Lord.

It is Jesus who sets before each succeeding generation the divinely ordained eternal triangle. As both husband and wife submit to him and draw closer to him, so they in reality draw closer to each other.

His lordship involves submission, and submission is the secret of blessing both in marriage and in every other aspect of our personal and corporate Christian lives.

# For personal reflection or group study

1 Have you consciously made Jesus Lord in your home and family? If not, is this a step you are able to take?
2 How can you best influence for Christ those members of the family or friends nearest to you?
3 Are there practical steps that your fellowship or church can take to help young people establish strong marriages 'in Christ'?

# EPILOGUE:
## 'EVEN SO, COME, LORD JESUS'

Throughout this book I have sought to demonstrate the unshakeably strong foundation upon which the claims of Jesus to be Lord are based. I have tried to show what it requires and what it results in for every area of our corporate church lives – our worship, leadership, mission and evangelism; our service as the body of Christ, our unity and our spiritual vitality; our fight against the forces of Satan and evil, and the growth of faith. I have also tried to show how personal commitment begins and flourishes. I have tried to illustrate by reference to many practical areas of life – the home and marriage, work and time and money, our emotions and reactions – the all-embracing nature of the lordship of Jesus.

My hope is that I shall have stimulated churches to re-establish the lordship of Jesus over their corporate life, as is his undoubted right, and to enter into all the blessings that this produces. I have tried to help each 'average' Christian understand and apply more fully the implications of the headship of Jesus in daily life.

I am also aware that there are still more aspects of our life which could have been covered in this book. For example, the final practical chapters could have dealt with the subjects of the Christian's attitude towards divorce, the need to work out a relevant Christian lifestyle for the end of the twentieth century and the application of Christ's lordship in the life of the single or widowed person – such issues as loneliness, independence and sexuality. Lack of space and competence means they must await another time.

What, however, cannot await another time or be in doubt is the glorious truth that the Lord Jesus will return one day.

I began the book with reference to one famous London landmark, St Paul's Cathedral. Let me conclude by referring to another. In the heart of Piccadilly is the renowned statue of Eros. It was erected in 1892, in memory of Anthony Ashley Cooper, the seventh Earl of Shaftesbury.

Lord Shaftesbury was a leading figure in the House of Commons and the House of Lords. He was the driving force behind the attempt to stop the exploitation of child labour in the nineteenth century, and also the visionary behind the establishment of many missionary, evangelistic and humanitarian societies still in existence today in Britain.

He is quoted as saying, 'I do not think that in the last forty years I have lived one conscious hour that was not influenced by the thought of our Lord's return.'[1]

Would that many more Christians had that testimony today! It is the assurance and the reality that the Lord will return which completes our understanding of his lordship.

It has been estimated that one in every thirteen verses of the new Testament is occupied with this fact. There are more references to the promised return of Jesus than to his first coming, and it is, not unnaturally, the major topic of the last book and last chapter of the Bible (Rev 22) to which I want to turn briefly.


## Jesus is revealed as Lord

Once again Jesus is revealed as Lord: 'I am the Alpha and the Omega, the First and the Last, the Beginning and the End' (Rev 22:13). Or again: 'I am the Root and the Offspring of David, and the bright Morning Star' (Rev 22:16).

Jesus takes to himself the divine names – 'Alpha' and 'Omega' – the first and last letters of the Greek alphabet. He is before everything, and he will sum up everything. He is the cause of all that is created and the fulfilment of all that exists. He is the beginning and the end.

Jesus also takes to himself the divine name: 'I am'. That

most ancient name given to God or taken by God – because it reflects his eternal and unchanging nature – is also taken by Jesus.

Jesus also refers to the fact that he is both an ancestor of David and a descendant from David. He comes before David and he follows on from David. He is claiming that he is the Lord of all history.

Jesus takes to himself the title of 'the bright Morning Star', a title that reflects the fact that he was there at the dawn of eternity and he will be there at the close of eternity.

Thus in a few words and titles, Jesus sums up for us that he is Lord of history, Lord of all human experience and Lord of heaven above.

## Jesus responded to as Lord

The remaining verses of this final chapter in the Bible spell out for us what it means to acknowledge that Jesus is Lord. We have already considered many of these truths.

○ We are called to obey his word and respond to it without adding anything to the word of God or taking anything away from it (vv.7,18–19)
○ We are called to worship him (v.9)
○ We are reminded that those who call him 'Lord' must live a holy life (vv.11,15)
○ We are required to witness to the truth and reality that he is Lord (v.10)
○ We are invited to share in his grace, and to live in harmony with his purposes (vv.14,17,21)
○ We are, above all, able to face the future with confidence. We have the conviction that Jesus as Lord has the future in his hands, that he is coming as he has promised, and that we may live as a people with hope and peace in our hearts

For the world watching and waiting at the end of the century, the future is unknown. Will there be nuclear disaster and explosion? Will there be the war to end all

wars? Will there be a great battle between East and West?
Will the rich get richer and the poor become poorer, and
millions die from famine and exposure?

The alternatives that are suggested by the world are too
awful to contemplate. But the Christian who acknowledges
that Jesus is Lord, even as he senses the end of the age
drawing near, knows he has the future in his hands and is
coming soon.

'"Yes, I am coming soon." Amen. Come, Lord Jesus'
(Rev 22:20). And until that time comes, we have been
assured that the grace of the Lord Jesus Christ will be with
God's people. So be it ('Amen') Lord.

## For personal reflection or group study

1 Do you really expect Jesus to return? What difference can this
  marvellous truth bring to our personal and church lives?
2 In what specific ways has the reading of *He is Lord* affected both
  your personal Christian life and your own local church life?

# NOTES

## 1 Jesus Christ is Lord

1 Ruskin, quoted in John R. W. Stott, *Basic Christianity* (IVP ²1971), p. 122.
2 E. W. Kenyon, *The Wonderful Name of Jesus* (Kenyon's Gospel Publishing Society 1964), p. 11.
3 Roy Pointer, *How Do Churches Grow?* (Marshalls 1984), p. 116.
4 'New life for the local church', *Renewal*, February–March 1986, pp. 11–12.
5 See, for example, A. M. Hodgkins, *Christ in All the Scriptures* (Marshalls 1986).
6 John R. W. Stott, *Issues Facing Christians Today* (Marshalls 1984), p. 16.
7 'Genesis' in D. and P. Alexander (eds), *The Lion Handbook to the Bible* (Lion Publishing 1973), p. 134.
8 Frank Colquhoun (ed.), *Parish Prayers* (Hodder & Stoughton 1967), p. 32.
9 John Eddison, *What Makes a Leader?* (Scripture Union 1974), p. 62.

## 2 Worship the Lord

1 Such as Graham Kendrick, *Worship* (Kingsway 1984); Michael Marshall, *Renewal in Worship* (Marshalls 1982); Andrew Maries, *One Heart, One Voice* (Hodder & Stoughton 1985).
2 Michael Marshall, *Renewal in Worship*, pp. 16–17.
3 Graham Kendrick, *Worship*, p. 94.
4 William Temple, *Citizen and Churchmen* (Eyre & Spottiswoode), p. 101.
5 Andrew Maries, *One Heart, One Voice*, p. 58.
6 William Barclay, *New Testament Words* (SCM Press 1964), pp. 176ff.
7 Paper from Rev. Terry Fulham, St Paul's Church, Darien, New York.

8 Graham Kendrick, *Worship*, p. 60.
9 William Temple, *Readings in St John's Gospel* (Macmillan 1939), p. 68.
10 Eddie Gibbs posed this question at a clergy conference I attended.
11 Graham Kendrick, *Worship*, p. 122.
12 ibid., p. 91.
13 Andrew Maries, *One Heart, One Voice*, p. 114.
14 The Music in Worship Trust, Director: Robin Sheldon, 151 Bath Road, Hounslow, Middlesex.
15 Private correspondence from Robin Sheldon, 27 February 1986.
16 William Hendriksen, *More Than Conquerors* (Tyndale Press 1962), p. 91.

## 3 Let the church hear his voice

1 J. D. Douglas (ed.), *Let the Earth Hear His Voice* (World Wide Publications 1975), the official report of the Lausanne Congress, 16–25 July 1974.
2 Michael Cole, *Prayer Changes People* (Marshalls 1986).
3 See also, Joyce Huggett, *Listening to God* (Hodder & Stoughton 1986).
4 The former Archbishop of York gave the Bible Readings at the South American Missionary Society Conference in Swanwick, April 1986.
5 A prophecy given at All Saints' Church, 19 January 1985.
6 John R. W. Stott, *Understanding the Bible* (Scripture Union 1972), esp. chapter 6.
7 Another book that fully covers the attitude of Christ to the Bible is: John W. Wenham, *Christ and the Bible* (Tyndale Press 1972), esp. chapters 1 and 5.
8 Oliver Styles, the leader of the Bude CSSM Beach Mission, August 1975.
9 W. E. Vine, *Expository Dictionary of New Testament Words* (1940; Marshalls 1981), p. 204.
10 We are grateful to John Truscott, the co-ordinator of Administry, 69 Sandridge Road, St Albans, Herts, for posing this question, following a survey of the parish.

# 4 One mind and one heart

1 Graham Kendrick, 'Jesus stand among us', in R. Fudge, P. Horrobin and G. Leavers (eds), *Mission Praise* (Marshalls 1983), number 124.
2 E. M. Blaiklock, *The Acts of the Apostles. An Introduction and Commentary*, Tyndale New Testament Commentaries (Tyndale Press 1959), p. 52.
3 J. Oswald Sanders, *Spiritual Leadership* (Marshalls 1967), p. 70.
4 ibid., p. 75.
5 John Perry, *Christian Leadership* (Hodder & Stoughton 1983), p. 80.
6 J. Oswald Sanders, *Spiritual Leadership*, p. 53.
7 Caleb, along with Joshua, wholly followed the Lord. Joshua 14:6–15 gives the account of Caleb receiving his inheritance because of his faithfulness.
8 The story of St Paul's, Darien, as recorded in Bob Slossor, *Miracle in Darien* (Logos International 1979).
9 ibid., p. 116.
10 'The way of peace', the November 1985 newsletter from The Rostrevor Renewal Centre, Ireland.


# 5 The challenge of mission

1 Quoted by Rev. Alan Flavelle in John Wallis (ed.), *We Believe in Mission* (Marshalls/STL 1983), p. 46.
2 The South American Missionary Society, Allen Gardiner House, Pembury Road, Tunbridge Wells, Kent, whose work in Latin and Central America, and the Iberian Peninsula, is supported in Britain, Australia, USA, Canada, New Zealand, South Africa and Ireland.
3 J. Oswald Sanders, *The Incomparable Christ* (Triangle 1982), p. 83.
4 Eddie Gibbs, *I Believe in Church Growth* (Hodder & Stoughton 1981), p. 121–122.
5 William Temple.
6 The experience of Gold Hill Baptist Church, quoted in Wallis (ed.), *We Believe in Mission*, pp. 146ff.

## 6 The clash of the kingdoms

1 See Michael Cole, *Prayer Changes People* (Marshalls 1986), pp. 89ff., where I have written more fully about the attacks of Satan.
2 Oscar Cullman, *Christ and Time* (Philadelphia: Westminster Press 1964), p. 84.
3 Christopher Koch, *The Year of Living Dangerously* (St Martin 1979).
4 Testimony of the Rev. Guy Catchpole, contained in a privately circulated memo entitled 'Freemasonry and Christianity'; used with permission.
5 See John Wimber, *Power Evangelism* (Hodder & Stoughton 1985) and *Power Healing* (Hodder & Stoughton 1986).
6 Clive Calver, *With a Church Like This . . . ?* (Marshalls 1981), p. 26.
7 ibid., p. ix.
8 Derek Prince's address to pastors in Singapore 1984.
9 Information about the Full Gospel Business Men's Fellowship International can be obtained from the UK Field Office: Elsterne, Toft Road, Knutsford, Cheshire WA16 9EB or from the World Headquarters: 3150 Bear Street, PO Box 5050, Costa Mesa, California 92626.

## 7 Serving the Lord

1 Martin Reardon's booklet, *What on Earth is the Church For?* (British Council of Churches 1986) formed the basis for the Lent Course 1986 and is available from the BCC at 2 Eaton Gate, London SW1W 9BL.
2 Jack Hayford, *The Church on the Way* (Chosen Books 1983), p. 167.
3 The electoral roll application form of the Church of England.
4 Keith Miller, *The Taste of New Wine* (Word Books 1965), p. 19.
5 Nigel Wright, 'Don't abdicate on the gifts', quoted in *Renewal* November 1986, from Acts 86 and Nigel Wright's workshop entitled 'The gifts of the Spirit'.
6 e.g., Selwyn Hughes, *Discovering Your Place in the Body of Christ* (Marshalls 1982), pp. 32–36. Also, The Department of Church Growth, Fuller Evangelistic Association, Box 989, Pasadena CA 91102.

7  C. Peter Wagner, *Your Spiritual Gifts Can Help Your Church Grow* (Regal Books 1979), p. 123.
8  ibid., p. 81.
9  Administry Resource Paper 86.2; quoted with permission.

## 8  The Spirit of the Lord

1  David Watson, *I Believe in the Church* (Hodder & Stoughton 1978), p. 166.
2  Michael Green, *I Believe in the Holy Spirit* (Hodder & Stoughton 1975), p. 39.
3  Canon James Wong, interviewed in *Prophecy Today* 2/1 (1986), pp. 30–31.
4  J. Edwin Orr, 'Search me, O God', in R. Fudge, P. Horrobin and G. Leavers (eds), *Mission Praise* (Marshalls 1983), number 200.
5  Galatians 3:1–5 from J. B. Phillips, *The New Testament in Modern English* (Geoffrey Bles 1960), p. 393.
6  *The Alternative Service Book 1980* (Hodder & Stoughton 1980), p. 145.

## 9  Increase our faith

1  William Barclay, *Hebrews*, Daily Study Bible (St Andrew's Press 1955), p. 144–145.
2  Ray Stedman, *What More Can God Say?* (Regal Books 1974), p. 182.
3  W. E. Vine, *Expository Dictionary of Bible Words* (1940; Marshalls 1981), p. 225.
4  Jean Darnall in *Renewal*, June–July 1985, p. 14.
5  Wesley, quoted in *Renewal*, June–July 1985, p. 9.
6  Basilea Schlink, *Realities* (Lakeland Books 1967), p. 36 (italics hers).
7  Jack R. Taylor, *The Hallelujah Factor* (Highland Books 1985), chapter 5, pp. 48–57.
8  Quoted in *Renewal*, June–July 1985, pp. 4–5.
9  Stanley H. Frodsham, *The Apostle of Faith. The Life of Smith Wigglesworth* (Assemblies of God 1949), pp. 33, 74.
10  Paul Billheimer, *Destined For the Throne* (Kingsway 1975), p. 18.

## 10 'My Lord and my God'

1 David Watson, *Discipleship* (Hodder & Stoughton 1981), p. 16.
2 W. E. Vine, *Expository Dictionary of Bible Words* (1940; Marshalls 1981), p. 316.
3 Jack R. Taylor, *The Hallelujah Factor* (Highland Books 1985), p. 50.
4 Roy Pointer, *How Do Churches Grow?* (Marshalls 1984), p. 117. Statement from Sale Baptist Church, Greater Manchester, England.
5 Jim Wallis, *The New Radical* (Lion Publishing 1983), p. 70.
6 ibid., p. 72.
7 J. C. Ryle, *Expository Thoughts on St John* (William Hunt & Co. 1873).
8 Watson, *Discipleship*, pp. 237–38.
9 John White, *The Cost of Commitment* (IVP 1976), pp. 20–21.


## 11 Total man

1 *The Christian Witness to the Jewish People*, Lausanne Occasional Paper 7 (Lausanne Committee for World Evangelization 1980), p. 22.
2 W. E. Vine, *Expository Dictionary of Bible Words* (1940; Marshalls 1981), p. 69.
3 Oliver Barclay, 'Loving God with all your mind' *Christian Arena*, June 1985, p. 18.
4 ibid.; italics his.
5 Jim Wallis, *The New Radical* (Lion Publishing 1983), p. 155.
6 Barbara Pursey, 'Healing is for the whole person', *Logos Journal* 1979, p. 23.
7 Donald Bridge, 'The Coming of Christ' in Ann England (ed.), *We Believe in Healing* (Marshalls 1982), p. 20.
8 James Dobson, *Emotions, Can You Trust Them?* (Hodder & Stoughton 1982), pp. 11–14.
9 Myra Chave-Jones, 'Be angry and sin not', Care and Counsel Paper 1977, p. 3.
10 R. G. V. Tasker, 'Wrath' in J. D. Douglas *et al.* (eds), *New Bible Dictionary* (IVP [2]1982), p. 1263.
11 James Dobson, *Emotions, Can You Trust Them?* p. 107.
12 ibid., 104.

13 James Dobson, *Hide or Seek* (Hodder & Stoughton 1974), pp. 27ff., 49ff.
14 Martyn Lloyd-Jones, *Studies in the Sermon on the Mount* I (IVP 1959), p. 109.
15 See Gordon Macdonald's *Living at High Noon – The Drama of Midlife* (MARC Europe 1986), chapter 5.

## 12 The world of work

1 William Barclay, *Letters to the Galatians and Ephesians*, Daily Study Bible (St Andrew Press ²1958), p. 215.
2 George Thomas, *Mr Speaker. The Memoirs of George Thomas* (Century Publishing 1985), p. 51.
3 Canon Paul Brett, The Chelmsford Diocesan Board of Social Responsibility Bulletin 6 (1986).
4 Gerry Griffin in the Spring 1986 newsletter of the Rostrevor Renewal Centre, Ireland.
5 See J. Oswald Sanders, *Enjoying Growing Old* (Kingsway 1981). In his book, Oswald Sanders writes very helpfully about the practical outworking of retirement for the Christian.

## 13 The pressure of time

1 Jenny Cooke, 'The frantic church', *Renewal* February–March 1986, p. 40.
2 John Lilley, 'Times and Seasons' in D. and P. Alexander (eds), *The Lion Handbook to the Bible* (Lion Publishing 1973), pp. 110–11.
3 Advent Sunday Collect from *The Alternative Service Book 1980* (Hodder & Stoughton 1980), p. 422.

## 14 Danger! Money

1 Richard Foster, *Money, Sex and Power* (Hodder & Stoughton 1985), p. 19.
2 ibid., p. 20.
3 ibid., chapters 2 and 3.
4 ibid., pp. 41–42.
5 ibid., pp. 44–46, 56–57.
6 ibid., p. 71; italics his.

## 15 Home is his castle

1 Eileen Vincent, *God Can Do It Here* (Marshalls 1982), pp. 41–42.
2 See John R. W. Stott, *Issues Facing Christians Today* (Marshalls 1984), chapter 13, 'Women, men and God'.
3 Among them, those by James Dobson and Tim LaHaye cover this area very well.
4 J. W. Meiklejohn, 'Barrenness' in J. D. Douglas *et al.* (eds), *New Bible Dictionary* (IVP ²1982), p. 125.
5 David Atkinson, *To Have and to Hold* (Collins 1979) and Stott, *Issues*, chapter 14, 'Marriage and Divorce'.
6 *The Book of Common Prayer* (OUP), p. 363.
7 *The Alternative Service Book 1980* (Hodder & Stoughton 1980), p. 288.

## Epilogue: 'Even so, come, Lord Jesus'

1 Stephen Travis, *The Jesus Hope* (Hodder & Stoughton 1983), p. 49.